BEYOND THE ACQUISITION

THRIVING WITH PRIVATE EQUITY OWNERSHIP

By Mort Greenberg

Copyright © 2025 by Mort Greenberg

Design and Illustrations: Heri Susanto

First Paperback edition April 2025

Print Paperback ISBN: 978-1-961059-19-1
Kindle KPF ISBN: 978-1-961059-20-7
Ingram EPUB ISBN: 978-1-961059-21-4

Published by digitalCORE
www.dgtlcore.com

digitalCORE

Other Books by Mort Greenberg

REVENUE VS. SALES SERIES

- **The Singular Focus**
  100+ Tips to Maximize Your Revenue

- **Revenue Boost**
  The Ultimate Sales Plan in Five Steps

- **Straight Up Selling**
  Your Toolbox for Sales Excellence

THE FOCUSED SELLER SERIES

- **Maximizing Human Performance in Sales**
  Unlocking Your Best Results By Thinking
  Like A Business Owner

- **The Sales Tactician**
  Spycraft Techniques for Revenue Success

- **Elevate**
  Mastering the Art of Sales Leadership

- **Beyond The Acquisition**
  Thriving With Private Equity Ownership

CHILDREN'S BOOK SERIES

The Fearless Girl and The Little Guy with Greatness

- **Book 1** - Live Life Motivated
- **Book 2** - Young Leaders Guide
- **Book 3** - Asking Awesome Questions
- **Book 4** - Think to Win
- **Book 5** - Smart Money Moves
- **Book 6** - Wellness Warriors
- **Book 7** - Travel Like a Pro
- **Book 8** - Outdoor Skills

To everyone that has taught me about business, thank you. And to those listed below who have shared their unique knowledge over the years, an extra thank you as your advice plays over and over in my head.

*To **MR** for inspiring excellence.*

*To **Kelly Facer** for operating with speed.*

*To **Doug Neiman** for deal creativity.*

*To **John Zayac** for giving time and counsel.*

*To **Keith Miller** for sharing experience.*

*To **Todd Brockman** for explaining the process.*

*To **Gen. David Petraeus (Ret.)** for continuous motivation.*

*To **George Bell** for infectious enthusiasm.*

*To **Bud Colligan** for calming wisdom.*

*To **Skip Battle** for never ending drive.*

*To **Mark Stein** for making it look easy.*

*To **Marjorie Weiss & Jim Martay** for printing ideas.*

*To **Peter A. Derow** for investing in people.*

*To **Dorothy Gemmell** for advice and guidance.*

*To **Kevin Dorsey** for positivity and caffeine.*

*To **Manny Alvarez** for always doubling down.*

This book is dedicated to each you!

FORWARD

For many of us, the private equity industry has been defined through the eyes of Hollywood. Movie after movie depicts larger than life characters, each living a life of excess, disrupting family run businesses for their own gain.

In truth, private equity firms have become an essential part our economy. Every day, private equity firms provide businesses of all sizes with a resource to meet their needs. Whether it be liquidity, technology, resources, or simply an exit strategy, private equity firms have become a vital outlet for business owners and investors alike.

In February of 2024, I witnessed the sale of a company to a private equity firm first-hand. As the founder of C-3 Technologies, a mid-size technical services company, I was approached by several private equity firms who were rolling up similar companies in my industry. Initially I was hesitant, but after careful consideration I agreed to explore the opportunity.

Several months later I found myself in due diligence. I was fortunate enough to have some friends who went through similar experiences, and although they were able to provide me with some advice on what to expect during the process, there were many times when I felt lost and frustrated.

Daily due diligence calls inevitably introduced me to any number of new acronyms while my financial privacy was laid bare for an army of 30 something professionals to judge. Day after day another hurdle was cleared, and as closing day approached, I eagerly anticipated the life of leisure I had spent a lifetime engineering. And then reality set in... the work was just beginning.

In his book, *Beyond The Acquisition*, Mort Greenberg provides a complete and comprehensive playbook for individuals who find themselves going through this process. His masterful explanation of the steps leading up to an acquisition is easily understandable and a must read for a business owner embarking on this path.

But where I found *Beyond The Acquisition* really stands out is the insight it provides for the post-acquisition transition. The process of integration can be uncomfortable and trying, but *Beyond The Acquisition* provides true and honest insight into the goals and objectives of private equity firms, and how they translate into initiatives that may seem unnecessary to those affected by it.

In my case, I quickly realized that those Gulf Coast sunsets would have to wait. It turned out that the post-closing environment for a founder was even more difficult than it is for the employees. On the one hand, it is imperative for a founder to provide stability and continuity for the staff, while on the other hand they must implement processes and procedures as dictated by the new management.

In *Beyond The Acquisition*, Mort provides insight and tools to effectively navigate and manage what is an extremely complicated time for employees and founders alike.

While private equity firms are not new, they have experienced a significant period of growth in the past few decades. Due to unusually low interest rates, investors have ventured out in search of better returns, and private equity has provided such an outlet. As a result, PE firms have become more aggressive and have become active in industries that we would not have imagined 20 years ago. Today we see private equity investing in all types of industries from technology to your local plumber.

Regardless of the industry, there is a good chance that founders or employees will embark on this journey at some point in their career. Whether you are a business owner in search of an exit, or an employee struggling to understand a rapidly changing environment, *Beyond The Acquisition* is an invaluable resource to succeed and flourish this demanding but exciting environment.

Manny Alvarez
Founder, C3 Technologies
Now a Proud Member
of Noble Fueling Solutions

INTRODUCTION

Welcome to *"Beyond The Acquisition: Thriving with Private Equity Ownership,"* the final installment of *"The Focused Seller"* series. This book is specifically crafted for business leaders, executives, and entrepreneurs who find themselves at the helm of a company undergoing or preparing for private equity acquisition. Here, you'll learn to navigate this new landscape with expertise, turning potential challenges into opportunities for substantial growth and success.

The journey through *"The Focused Seller"* series has equipped you with a robust set of skills and strategies. Starting with *"Maximizing Human Performance In Sales: Unlocking Your Best Results By Thinking Like A Business Owner,"* you developed the foundational skills necessary for individual sales excellence and an understanding of the business owner's mindset. *"The Sales Tactician: Spycraft Techniques for Revenue Success"* then advanced your tactical capabilities, employing espionage-inspired strategies for intricate deal-making and client interactions. In *"Elevate: Mastering the Art of Sales Leadership,"* you were prepared to take on greater responsibility, learning to inspire and lead teams with visionary insight.

Now, in *"Beyond The Acquisition,"* the focus shifts to thriving in the complex and often high-stakes environment of private equity ownership. This book will guide you through managing the critical first 100 days post-acquisition, aligning with new ownership objectives, fostering innovation, and driving growth to maximize the value of your enterprise. You'll also explore strategies for scaling your business, leveraging networks, and preparing for future exits—skills that are crucial for sustaining success in the fast-paced private equity world.

Each book in this series builds upon the last, forming a pathway from individual sales proficiency to strategic business management under the unique pressures of private equity. *"Beyond The Acquisition"* not only culminates this series but also provides the crucial tools needed for senior leaders to navigate and succeed in this specialized business environment.

You, the reader are an Operator, and as you know, change is the only constant in business. If you are taking the time to read this book, you are willing to become a positive change agent for your company.

When a private equity firm steps in, the stakes get higher, and the speed of change accelerates. But it also presents a unique opportunity for individuals and organizations to grow, scale, and become more competitive.

Over the past eight years I have worked as a business operator inside of a PE firm where my focus is on improving distressed media companies. As you can imagine, I have witnessed firsthand the challenges and opportunities that come with such transitions. This book seeks to equip you with the knowledge, mindset, and strategies to thrive under new ownership.

Before we get into the core of the book, here are seven key items to start thinking about. This Cheat sheet is a good baseline to keep coming back to as you read the pages ahead:

1. **Clarify the New Leadership Vision:** Ensure you understand the goals and strategic direction of the private equity firm, and communicate this clearly to your team to align everyone with the new priorities.

2. **Focus on the First 100 Days:** Use the critical first 100 days to establish trust with the new owners, set clear expectations, and stabilize the business. Immediate action and strong communication during this period are key.

3. **Aggressively Manage the Transition Services Agreement (TSA):** Daily project management of the TSA will best

optimize processes key systems, and infrastructure you are acquiring around IT, HR, finance, logistics and more.

4. **Prioritize Performance Metrics:** Identify the key performance metrics (like expenses, profits, revenue growth, and cash flow from operations) that the PE firm cares about, and align your team's efforts around hitting these targets.

5. **Optimize Operations:** Look for quick operational wins to improve efficiency, reduce costs, and optimize workflows. Implement process improvements or technology upgrades to streamline operations.

6. **Retain Key Talent:** Quickly build org charts and identify the least number of key people that you can run the business with. Offer retention packages or incentives to keep critical personnel engaged. Make sure key employees feel valued and understand how their roles fit into the company's future.

7. **Encourage Innovation:** Foster a culture of innovation by supporting disruptive thinking and encouraging employees to propose new ideas that can drive growth and competitive advantage.

Focus Area	Checklist Items	Metrics to Monitor
Clarify the New Leadership Vision	1. Assign Leadership Alignment Tasks 2. Develop a Communication Plan 3. Create Strategic Priorities 4. Ensure Leadership Buy-In 5. Update Company Mission and Goals	1. Create and send out various surveys 2. Engagement metrics from town halls, email open rates 3. Percentage of Leadership Buy-In 4. Completion of Mission updates
Focus on the First 100 Days	1. Assign Immediate Action Items 2. Monitor Financial Performance	1. Completion of key milestones (30/60/100 days) 2. Revenue, expenses, and cash flow reports

Focus Area	Checklist Items	Metrics to Monitor
Focus on the First 100 Days	3. Communicate Regularly with New Owners 4. Evaluate and Adjust Leadership Roles 5. Address Immediate employee Concerns	3. Number of successful check-ins with owners 4. Timely leadership assessments 5. Employee feedback or surveys
Aggressively Manage the TSA	1. Appoint TSA Managers 2. Set Clear TSA Deliverables 3. Hold Daily Progress Meetings 4. Monitor Costs Associated with TSA 5. Establish Exit Plan from TSA	1. Daily TSA Progress reports 2. Completion Percentage of TSA Deliverables 3. TSA cost vs. budget 4. Percentage of TSA phase-outs
Prioritize Performance Metrics	1. Identify key Financial metrics 2. Set Growth Targets 3. Track Expense Reduction 4. Monitor Cash Flow from Operations 5. Ensure Accountability for metrics	1. Monthly/quarterly revenue, EBITDA, Cash Flow 2. Revenue Growth Percentage MoM/YoY 3. Expense Reduction Percentage 4. Liquidity ratios 5. Performance Targets met
Optimize Operations	1. Conduct a Quick Operational Audit 2. Implement cost-Saving Measures 3. Invest In Technology Upgrades 4. Improve Workflow Processes 5. Track Efficiency Gains	1. Completion of Operational Audit 2. Monthly cost-Saving reports 3. Operational Efficiency metrics, Technology ROI 4. Process improvements 5. Productivity and throughput metrics
Retain Key Talent	1. Identify key Personnel 2. Design Retention Packages 3. Communicate Future Opportunities 4. Build New Org Charts 5. Monitor employee Engagement	1. Retention rate of key Personnel 2. Number of Retention agreements 3. Employee satisfaction and Engagement scores 4. Completion of New organizational structure 5. Monthly Engagement survey results

Focus Area	Checklist Items	Metrics to Monitor
Encourage Innovation	1. Create an Innovation Team 2. Establish Innovation Channels 3. Set Innovation Goals 4. Provide Resources for R&D 5. Track Innovation ROI	1. Number of ideas generated and implemented 2. Idea submission rate 3. Innovation goals achieved 4. R&D spend vs. output 5. ROI on innovation

Embark on the final leg of your journey with *"Beyond The Acquisition: Thriving with Private Equity Ownership"* and prepare to transform your approach to leadership and strategic management in the private equity context. This book is your guide to not just surviving but thriving in the new dynamics that private equity brings to your professional life and your organization.

AUTHOR'S NOTE

Believe in Possibility and Understand The Power of Cash Flow

When a company is acquired by private equity, the immediate reaction from employees ranges from excitement to uncertainty. But regardless of the initial feelings, one principle that becomes the cornerstone of post-acquisition success is getting team members to believe that they can influence change and growth.

Everyone has ideas and opinions that need to be heard. And it is critical to make sure all have a voice as early into the acquisition as possible. Creating culture is not easy. But making sure each employee feels like they are being listened to is the first step. And, just as important as listening to staff can be, is letting the Private Equity owners know that you are focused on their needs. And those needs are revenue generation and cash flow

Revenue is the lifeblood of any company and sales is the process to generate revenue. Revenue is what fuels expansion, attracts new customers, and validates the market's demand for your product or service. However, without a straightforward focus on sales, even the most promising opportunities can be missed. One of the most important things to focus on after a PE acquisition is optimizing the monetization engine—ensuring it's not only scalable but also consistently delivering predictable outcomes. Private equity firms expect results, and this starts with a process that can find the right leads and convert into revenue reliably.

However, revenue alone isn't enough. Cash flow is the heartbeat that keeps the company running smoothly.

Healthy, predictable cash flow allows for flexibility, makes strategic investments possible, and gives the company room to grow. It also provides confidence to your new PE owners that the business is on the right track. Without a solid understanding of your cash flow and how to manage it, even the best revenue numbers can't guarantee success.

The most successful post-acquisition companies are those where every employee–from leadership to frontline staff–embraces the belief that they can contribute to revenue growth and cash flow management. They understand that every deal closed, every customer retained, and every process improved can add value to the business in tangible ways.

The magic happens when employees not only believe in this potential but are empowered to act on it. When sales teams are fine-tuned, operations are aligned with growth, and finance is laser-focused on cash flow management, you create an unstoppable momentum.

It's not just about survival in a post-acquisition environment– it's about thriving. And that starts with the belief that every employee has a voice, there is a focus on revenue and cash flow, and that will create the best outcome for all involved.

Mort Greenberg

SECTIONS AND CHAPTERS

UNDERSTANDING PRIVATE EQUITY AND THE BUYOUT PROCESS

In order to thrive after a private equity (PE) buyout, it's crucial to first understand the driving forces behind PE, how these firms operate, and what they're aiming to achieve. For employees and leaders alike, knowledge of the fundamental workings of private equity will provide invaluable context. It's not just about grasping financial mechanisms or investment strategies but about realizing how these elements impact every decision made post-acquisition— from budget allocations to growth targets and cultural shifts.

In this section, we will dive deep into the world of private equity: its history, how PE firms function, and why businesses become acquisition targets. We'll explore the different types of PE investments and what these variations mean for a company post-buyout. Gaining clarity on these topics sets the foundation for navigating and thriving under new ownership. This understanding will be essential as the story of the company evolves in the hands of its new PE owners.

CHAPTER 1

What Is Private Equity?

"

Understanding private equity is the first step to unlocking a future of strategic growth, innovation, and new opportunities for your business.

"

History and Evolution of Private Equity

Private equity, as we know it today, has its roots in the early 20th century. It began as a loosely defined area of finance, focusing on investing in private companies, as opposed to publicly traded ones, and evolved into one of the most powerful forces in the global economy. The modern private equity industry has grown tremendously since its inception, and understanding how it got here can provide valuable insight into the way it operates today.

In the 1940s and 1950s, the early forms of private equity were closely tied to venture capital, with investors seeking high-risk, high-reward opportunities in early-stage companies. The post-World War II boom gave rise to numerous private investment firms that specialized in injecting capital into growing businesses. In the 1980s, the landscape of private equity changed dramatically with the rise of leveraged buyouts (LBOs), a mechanism where firms would acquire companies using a combination of equity and significant amounts of borrowed funds. This allowed private equity firms to make massive investments while minimizing their own capital at risk.

The 1980s also saw the birth of some of the largest and most well-known PE firms, like Kohlberg Kravis Roberts (KKR) and The Carlyle Group, both of which perfected the LBO strategy and made headlines with high-profile deals. These firms demonstrated how private equity could not only drive significant returns for investors but also fundamentally reshape the companies they acquired, sometimes through aggressive restructuring or operational overhauls.

As the years passed, private equity expanded its horizons, moving beyond LBOs to other strategies like growth capital, mezzanine financing, and distressed asset investing. By the 2000s, PE had become a major player in global mergers and acquisitions (M&A), handling not just company buyouts but also contributing to large-scale restructurings, roll-ups, and transformative initiatives across various industries. The post-financial crisis period from 2008 onward saw private equity firms taking on even greater roles in revitalizing struggling companies, offering innovative strategies to turn around businesses hit hard by recession.

Today, private equity firms control trillions of dollars in assets and have a profound influence on nearly every industry. From tech startups to industrial giants, the impact of private equity is felt across the global economy. Understanding this history helps illuminate the motives and strategies PE firms bring to the table when they acquire companies.

How PE Firms Operate: Structure and Investment Strategy

At its core, a private equity firm is a financial entity that pools capital from institutional investors, such as pension funds, endowments, and high-net-worth individuals, with the goal of making investments in private companies. These firms typically operate through funds, where investors contribute capital over a defined period. The general partners (GPs) of the firm are responsible for identifying investment opportunities, managing portfolio companies, and ultimately delivering strong returns to their limited partners (LPs), who are the outside investors.

The lifecycle of a PE firm's involvement with a company generally follows a structured approach:

1. **Fundraising:** Private equity firms raise capital from LPs in cycles, creating funds with a specific target size. This could range from a few hundred million to several billion dollars. The firm will aim to deploy this capital over a few years while generating returns through eventual exits (e.g., selling or taking companies public).

2. **Deal Sourcing and Acquisition:** Once a fund is raised, the firm focuses on sourcing deals—identifying potential companies to acquire. PE firms typically look for companies that are underperforming, have growth potential, or can benefit from operational improvements. After identifying targets, they structure the deal, which often includes a mix of equity and debt (the leveraged buyout model).

3. **Value Creation:** After the acquisition, the PE firm takes an active role in managing the company. They work closely with the management team to improve operations, streamline costs, drive revenue growth, and sometimes change leadership. The goal during this period is to increase the company's value significantly.

4. **Exit Strategy:** Once value has been created, PE firms look to exit their investment. This can take place through a sale to another company, a sale to another private equity firm, or through an initial public offering (IPO). The goal is to maximize the return on investment, ideally achieving a multiple of the initial capital deployed.

PE firms are often organized into teams with distinct roles, including deal origination, operational improvement, and financial engineering. Deal origination professionals focus on finding potential targets, while operational experts work to improve portfolio companies, and financial engineers design capital structures that optimize returns for investors. The combination of these roles makes private equity firms highly specialized and effective in transforming businesses.

Types of Private Equity Investments

While the term "private equity" is often used to describe a broad category of investment, there are multiple types of investments within this space, each with its own goals and strategies:

1. Leveraged Buyouts (LBOs):

This is the most well-known form of private equity investment, where a firm acquires a company using a combination of equity and significant debt. The company's vcash flow is used to service the debt over time, with the goal of eventually selling the company at a profit.

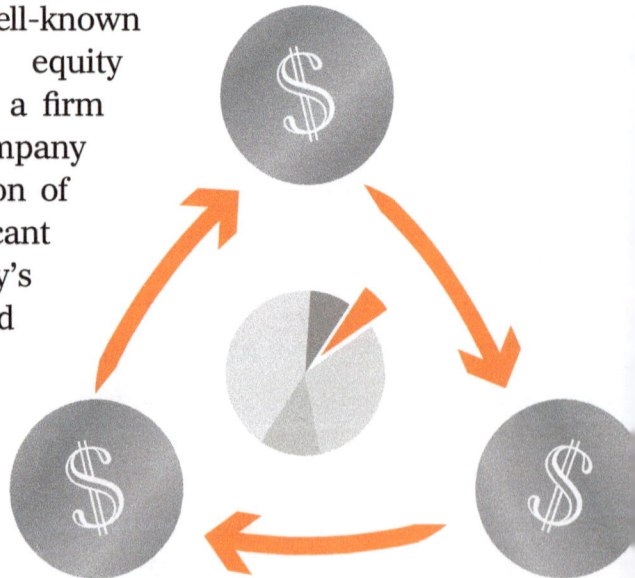

2. **Growth Capital:** Growth capital investments focus on companies that are beyond the startup phase but still need capital to expand. Unlike LBOs, growth capital investments typically don't involve significant debt. Instead, the private equity firm provides funds to fuel growth, often by helping the company enter new markets, build new products, or increase operational capacity.

3. **Venture Capital (VC):** Venture capital is technically a subset of private equity, though it operates in a different realm. VC firms invest in early-stage companies with high growth potential, particularly in industries like technology and biotech. These investments are riskier, as they often involve companies without established track records.

4. **Distressed Asset Investing:** In this type of investment, PE firms acquire companies or assets that are under financial distress, such as those near bankruptcy. The goal is to turn the company around through restructuring, operational improvements, or a complete overhaul.

5. **Mezzanine Financing:** This is a hybrid form of investment that combines debt and equity financing. Mezzanine financing is typically used by companies looking to raise capital without giving up control, as it allows for capital infusion while still servicing debt.

6. **Roll-Ups:** A roll-up strategy involves acquiring multiple smaller companies within a fragmented industry and consolidating them into a larger, more competitive entity. This approach creates economies of scale, synergies, and potentially more market dominance.

Each type of private equity investment involves a different risk and reward profile, and PE firms often specialize in one or more of these strategies. Understanding the type of private equity investment a company is subject to can help employees and leadership better align their actions with the firm's goals.

Explore Types of Private Equity Investments

Objective: Familiarize yourself with the different types of private equity investments and their applications.

Instructions:

- Create a list of different types of private equity investments from Chapter 1, such as:
  - » Buyouts (majority stake acquisitions)
  - » Growth equity (minority stake investments in growing companies)
  - » Venture capital (early-stage investments)
  - » Distressed investments (turnarounds)
- Research recent real-world examples of each type of investment (either individually or in small groups) and answer the following questions:
  - » What was the PE firm's strategy for the investment?
  - » What stage was the target company in when the investment was made?
  - » How did the firm create value for the company?

Output: Do a write up of each type of PE investment works and how value is created.

Actionable Takeaway: This activity will help you differentiate between various PE investment strategies and the contexts in which they are most effective.

Conclusion

Private equity is a diverse and powerful force in today's business world. Its history, structure, and various investment strategies shape how these firms approach acquisitions and the companies they buy. For those within the acquired business, understanding the fundamentals of private equity is the first step toward navigating this new chapter effectively. Knowing how PE firms create value and what they prioritize can position individuals and teams to align with the new objectives and thrive under their guidance. In the following chapters, we'll explore how these principles play out during the post-acquisition phase and how to manage the transition effectively.

CHAPTER 2

The Buyout Process Unveiled

━━━━━━━━━━━━ 66 ━━━━━━━━━━━━

A successful buyout is not just about financial engineering—it's about creating a roadmap to long-term value and resilience.

━━━━━━━━━━━━ 99 ━━━━━━━━━━━━

Private equity (PE) acquisitions are complex, multi-step transactions that involve a range of strategic, financial, and operational considerations. For businesses being acquired, understanding the stages of this process is crucial to navigating the transition successfully. A private equity buyout is not simply the sale of a company; it's a carefully orchestrated series of events designed to maximize value for both the acquiring firm and the company itself.

In this chapter, we will take an in-depth look at the key stages of a private equity buyout, the rigorous due diligence process that PE firms use to evaluate targets, and the financial tools PE firms employ to structure these deals for optimal returns. This understanding will empower employees and leaders of acquired companies to anticipate the key milestones and adapt effectively to the changes that come with PE ownership.

Stages of a PE Acquisition

The process of a private equity acquisition can be broken down into several key stages, each of which plays a critical role in determining the success of the transaction. These stages include deal sourcing, negotiation, due diligence, transaction structuring, closing, and post-acquisition management.

1. Deal Sourcing and Initial Evaluation

The first stage in any PE acquisition is deal sourcing. Private equity firms are constantly on the lookout for potential investment opportunities, typically through networks of investment bankers, brokers, industry experts, and their own deal origination teams. PE firms will also proactively seek out companies that fit their investment criteria, focusing on industries where they have expertise or see growth potential.

Deal sourcing is highly competitive, with PE firms often vying for the same high-quality assets. As a result, companies that are potential acquisition targets are thoroughly evaluated in this stage based on financial performance, market position, and growth potential. PE firms typically look for companies that are either underperforming (and can benefit from operational improvements) or have significant upside potential with the right strategic guidance and capital infusion.

2. Initial Negotiation and Terms Agreement

Once a target company is identified and initial discussions are underway, the next step is to enter into preliminary negotiations. At this stage, the PE firm will engage with the company's leadership or its owners to discuss the terms of a potential deal. This includes agreeing on the price range, key deal terms, and general strategic goals for the transaction.

During this phase, the parties will usually sign a **letter of intent (LOI)** or a **memorandum of understanding (MOU)** that outlines the terms of the proposed transaction, including the price and any exclusivity arrangements. The LOI is non-binding but provides a framework for the due diligence process and more detailed negotiations that follow.

3. Due Diligence

Due diligence is one of the most critical stages of a private equity acquisition. In this phase, the PE firm conducts a thorough review of the target company's financials, operations, legal standing, and market position. The goal is to ensure that the company is a sound investment and that there are no hidden risks that could undermine the deal's success. Due diligence typically covers the following areas:

- **Financial Due Diligence:** PE firms will comb through the company's financial statements, tax records, and key performance indicators (KPIs) to assess its financial health. They look for revenue trends, profitability margins, and cash flow stability. Financial due diligence also involves evaluating the company's balance sheet, identifying any debt obligations, and analyzing working capital requirements.

- **Operational Due Diligence:** In addition to financial scrutiny, PE firms will evaluate the company's operational efficiency. This includes analyzing production processes, supply chain management, inventory controls, and the scalability of operations. The goal here is to determine whether the company can support growth initiatives and where improvements can be made to drive higher margins.

- **Legal Due Diligence:** Legal risks can significantly impact the value of a company, which is why PE firms will engage legal counsel to review the company's contracts, litigation history, intellectual property, regulatory compliance, and employment agreements. Any legal issues or liabilities must be identified and factored into the transaction's terms.

- **Market Due Diligence:** Finally, the PE firm will assess the target company's market position and competitive landscape. This involves reviewing the company's customer base, market share, industry trends, and potential threats from competitors. The goal is to verify the company's growth potential and alignment with the PE firm's strategic objectives.

Due diligence is often conducted over a period of several weeks or even months, depending on the complexity of the deal. PE firms will rely on a team of accountants, lawyers, and industry experts to ensure that they have a complete understanding of the company before proceeding with the transaction.

4. Deal Structuring and Financing

After due diligence, the next stage is to finalize the deal structure. This is where private equity firms employ various financial tools and strategies to optimize the transaction for both risk and return. One of the most common mechanisms used by PE firms is the leveraged buyout (LBO), where a significant portion of the acquisition is financed with debt.

In an LBO, the PE firm uses a combination of its own equity and borrowed funds to finance the acquisition. The debt is typically secured against the assets of the target company and is serviced through the company's future cash flows. This structure allows PE firms to minimize their equity investment while maximizing potential returns.

The deal structure will also outline other key terms, such as the ownership stake the PE firm will hold, the company's future governance structure, and any performance-based incentives for the management team. In many cases, existing shareholders or management may retain a minority stake in the company, aligning their interests with the PE firm's objectives.

5. Closing the Deal

Once the deal structure is finalized and financing is secured, the next step is to close the transaction. This involves completing all legal formalities, transferring ownership, and executing any required changes in the company's governance structure. Closing can be a lengthy process, particularly if regulatory approvals are needed, or if the deal involves multiple jurisdictions.

At closing, the private equity firm takes control of the company, and any new management or operational changes are typically put into motion. This is the official handover point, where the company begins its new chapter under private equity ownership.

6. Post-Acquisition Management and Value Creation

The final stage of a PE acquisition is the post-acquisition management phase, where the private equity firm works closely with the company's leadership to implement its strategic plan. This phase is all about driving value creation—

through operational improvements, revenue growth, cost savings, or strategic acquisitions.

PE firms often bring in their own teams of operational experts, who work with the company to optimize processes, improve margins, and scale the business. In some cases, this involves a significant restructuring of the company, including changes in leadership, workforce reductions, or divestitures of non-core assets.

The goal during this phase is to increase the company's overall value, setting the stage for a profitable exit, typically within three to seven years. PE firms will monitor key performance metrics closely during this period, making adjustments to their strategy as necessary to maximize returns.

Due Diligence:

What PE Firms Look For

Due diligence is the cornerstone of any private equity acquisition. It provides the acquiring firm with the information it needs to make an informed investment decision and to identify any potential risks or opportunities associated with the target company. This process is typically divided into several key categories, each of which plays an essential role in determining the final terms of the deal.

Financial Due Diligence

Financial due diligence is arguably the most critical aspect of the process. Private equity firms are looking for companies that can generate strong returns, which means they need a deep understanding of the target's financial health and future prospects. The key areas of focus include:

- **Revenue Streams:** PE firms assess the stability and predictability of the company's revenue streams. Are revenues concentrated in a few key customers, or is the customer base diverse? Is revenue recurring, or does it depend on one-time sales?

- **Profitability Margins:** PE firms scrutinize the company's gross margins, operating margins, and net income to understand its profitability. Companies with healthy margins are more attractive, as they offer greater potential for operational improvement and cost optimization.

- **Cash Flow:** Cash flow is a critical metric for private equity firms, as it determines the company's ability to service debt and fund growth initiatives. PE firms look for strong, predictable cash flow that can support leveraged financing.

- **Debt Levels:** PE firms evaluate the company's existing debt obligations to ensure they are manageable post-acquisition. High levels of debt can limit the company's ability to grow and can increase financial risk.

- **Working Capital:** Working capital management is another key focus. PE firms want to ensure that the company has enough liquidity to meet its short-term obligations without sacrificing long-term growth.

Operational Due Diligence

In addition to financial due diligence, PE firms conduct a thorough review of the company's operations. The goal is to identify areas where the company can become more efficient, scale its operations, or reduce costs. Key areas of focus include:

- **Supply Chain:** PE firms assess the company's supply chain to ensure it is efficient, reliable, and scalable. They look for opportunities to streamline procurement, reduce lead times, and optimize inventory management.

- **Production Processes:** PE firms evaluate the company's production processes to identify inefficiencies and potential areas for improvement. This includes analyzing labor costs, equipment utilization, and production throughput.

- **Technology and Systems:** Technology plays a critical role in modern business operations. PE firms assess the company's IT infrastructure, software systems, and digital capabilities to determine whether they are aligned with growth objectives.

Legal and Regulatory Due Diligence

Legal due diligence is another key component of the process. PE firms want to ensure that the company is in compliance with all applicable laws and regulations, and that there are no outstanding legal issues that could pose a risk to the transaction. Key areas of focus include:

- **Contracts:** PE firms review the company's contracts with customers, suppliers, employees, and other stakeholders to ensure they are favorable and enforceable.

- **Litigation History:** PE firms evaluate the company's litigation history to identify any ongoing or potential legal disputes that could impact its financial performance or reputation.

- **Regulatory Compliance:** PE firms assess the company's compliance with industry regulations, environmental laws, and labor standards. Non-compliance can result in fines, penalties, and reputational damage.

Financial Engineering: Understanding the Tools Used by PE

Financial engineering is one of the most powerful tools in the private equity playbook. It involves structuring the deal in a way that maximizes returns while minimizing risk. PE firms use a variety of financial strategies to achieve this, including leveraged buyouts (LBOs), recapitalizations, and dividend recapitalizations.

Leveraged Buyouts (LBOs)

The leveraged buyout is the most common tool used by private equity firms to acquire companies. In an LBO, the PE firm uses a combination of its own equity and borrowed funds to finance the acquisition. The debt is typically secured against the company's assets and is serviced through the company's future cash flows.

Recapitalization

Recapitalization involves restructuring the company's debt and equity mix to optimize its capital structure. This can involve issuing new equity, repurchasing existing equity, or refinancing debt.

Workshop Activities

Objective: This checklist will provide buyers with a comprehensive understanding of the business they are acquiring and ensure they make informed decisions during the due diligence process. See the sample checklist below to get you started.

Instructions:

Develop 3-5 questions for each selected focus area that would help you gather additional information or clarify any uncertainties.

Output: What essential documents/data would you request for each focus area? What critical questions would you develop to gather more information? Where are the potential risks or red flags in the business? What key metrics would you use to monitor / assess the business post-acquisition?

Actionable Takeaway: By completing this activity, you will gain practical experience in conducting due diligence for a business acquisition.

Focus Area	Checklist Items	Metrics to Monitor
Business Overview	1. Business structure and history 2. Ownership and governance 3. Industry and market analysis	1. Market share and SWOT 2. Competitor analysis 3. Employee alignment with new Ownership

Focus Area	Checklist Items	Metrics to Monitor
Financials	1. Financial statements (3-5 years) 2. Profitability by product/service 3. Cash flow forecast	1. Revenue growth, EBITDA 2. Cash flow from operations 3. Profit margins and debt levels
Staff and Human Resources	1. Complete list of employees 2. Employee agreements and benefits 3. Succession planning	1. Employee turnover rate 2. Retention of key personnel 3. Employee satisfaction and engagement
Systems and Technology	1. IT infrastructure and systems 2. CRM and customer data management 3. Software licenses	1. System uptime and security 2. Data privacy compliance (GDPR, CCPA) 3. Efficiency of IT systems
Customers and Sales	1. List of top customers and contracts for past 3 years, updated monthly until close 2. Sales pipeline and customer segmentation 3. Customer Retention	1. Customer retention rate 2. Sales growth (monthly/annual) 3. Customer acquisition cost (CAC)
Legal and Compliance	1. Corporate documents and contracts 2. Ongoing/past litigation 3. Regulatory compliance	1. Legal compliance 2. Outstanding liabilities 3. Regulatory and compliance issues resolved
Operations and Supply Chain	1. Supply chain contracts 2. Production/service processes 3. Facility and real estate information	1. Inventory turnover rate 2. Supply chain risks and disruptions 3. Facility utilization and maintenance

Focus Area	Checklist Items	Metrics to Monitor
Growth Opportunities and Strategic Initiatives	1. Current growth areas 2. R&D and product development 3. Expansion plans	1. New product revenue contribution 2. ROI on R&D initiatives 3. Market entry success metrics
Risk Management and Insurance	1. Insurance policies and coverage 2. Business continuity plans 3. Operational and IT risks	1. Claims history 2. Disaster recovery readiness 3. Risk management effectiveness

Conclusion

By comprehensively understanding the roles and expectations in a PE acquisition, companies can better prepare for success under new ownership, ensuring a smoother transition and a more prosperous future under the strategic guidance of their private equity partners. This chapter has provided the roadmap for understanding and navigating this complex process, empowering businesses to thrive in the dynamic world of private equity acquisitions.

CHAPTER 3

Why Companies Are Acquired by Private Equity

---- 66 ----

Private equity sees potential where others may not—align your company's strengths to become the next strategic acquisition.

---- 99 ----

Private equity firms target companies with potential for significant growth, operational improvements, or strategic transformations. This chapter explores acquisition triggers, desired growth, strategic value, and signs a company may attract private equity interest. Understanding these factors enables business owners and managers to comprehend why their company is appealing, how to prepare for acquisition, and how to maximize value in potential deals. By recognizing what drives private equity interest, companies can strategically position themselves within the private equity ecosystem for optimal outcomes.

Common Triggers
for PE Interest

Private equity firms don't acquire companies on a whim. They have specific criteria and strategic objectives when seeking investment opportunities. These criteria are often centered around the potential for value creation, operational improvements, or strategic growth initiatives. While every PE firm may have its own approach, several common triggers tend to attract their attention.

1. Underperformance Relative to Potential

One of the most common reasons private equity firms acquire companies is because they believe the business is underperforming relative to its potential. This could mean the company is not maximizing its operational efficiency, not fully utilizing its assets, or not achieving the growth it could under different management.

PE firms see underperformance as an opportunity. With the right leadership, strategic direction, and operational improvements, they can unlock the company's potential and create significant value. These firms often look for businesses where they can step in and make rapid improvements through cost-cutting, process optimization, or enhanced revenue generation strategies.

Signs of underperformance that may attract PE interest include:

- Declining or stagnant revenue growth despite a strong market position

- Inefficiencies in production or service delivery that lead to higher operating costs

- Excessive overhead or bloated administrative structures
- Poor management of working capital, leading to cash flow issues

2. Succession or Ownership Transitions

Many companies become attractive targets for private equity when they are undergoing or preparing for ownership transitions. This is particularly true for family-owned businesses or companies with aging leadership, where the next generation of leadership may not be interested or capable of taking over.

Private equity firms often step in during these transitions because they can offer an orderly exit for existing owners while providing the capital and expertise needed to continue growing the business. This type of acquisition is appealing because the business itself may be healthy and profitable but requires new leadership to guide it into its next phase of growth.

PE firms are especially drawn to businesses where:

- The founders or majority owners are looking to retire or step back
- There is no clear succession plan in place
- The company is transitioning from private or family ownership to a more corporate structure

3. Need for Capital to Fund Growth

Another common reason for private equity acquisition is the need for significant capital to fund expansion. Many companies have the potential to grow rapidly but are limited by a lack of access to capital. Whether it's opening new locations, investing in research and development, or expanding into new markets, companies often require large sums of money to execute on their growth plans.

PE firms provide both the capital and the strategic expertise to help companies scale efficiently and sustainably. This is particularly attractive for companies that have hit a growth ceiling but have a clear path forward with the right funding. PE firms may also offer access to their networks, providing strategic partnerships or other resources to accelerate growth.

Some scenarios where capital needs may attract PE interest include:

- The need for capital-intensive investments, such as new manufacturing facilities or technology upgrades

- Expansion into international markets that require significant upfront investment

- Mergers and acquisitions that require financial backing

- Product development initiatives that need substantial research and development (R&D) funding

4. Industry Consolidation or Fragmentation

Private equity firms are also drawn to industries that are either consolidating or highly fragmented. In the case of industry consolidation, PE firms look for opportunities to acquire smaller companies and roll them up into a larger entity, thereby gaining market share and achieving economies of scale. This strategy is particularly common in industries where there are many small players and where consolidation can lead to stronger competitive positioning.

In fragmented industries, PE firms see the potential to build a dominant player by acquiring several smaller companies and integrating them under one umbrella. This approach, known as a "roll-up strategy," allows PE firms to create a company that can command greater pricing power, improve operational efficiencies, and achieve better bargaining positions with suppliers and customers.

Industries that are ripe for consolidation or fragmentation may exhibit:

- Many small or regional players competing for the same customers

- Opportunities to achieve significant cost savings or synergies through consolidation

- Markets where larger competitors are gaining market share by acquiring smaller players

5. Strong Growth Potential in a Niche Market

Private equity firms often target companies that are operating in niche markets with strong growth potential. These companies may be small or mid-sized, but they dominate their specific market segment or have a unique value proposition that differentiates them from larger competitors.

PE firms are particularly interested in niche companies that have high barriers to entry, such as specialized technology, intellectual property, or deep customer relationships. These companies may have significant growth potential, either by expanding their product offerings, entering new geographic markets, or capitalizing on emerging trends within their industry.

Niche markets that attract PE interest often have:

- High levels of customer loyalty and long-term contracts

- Strong competitive advantages that are difficult for other players to replicate

- Opportunities for expansion beyond the core business, such as complementary product lines or services

Growth Potential
and Strategic Value

While every private equity firm has its own approach to evaluating potential acquisitions, one factor that consistently drives PE interest is the company's growth potential and strategic value. Private equity firms are in the business of creating value, and they do this by identifying companies that have untapped growth opportunities or that can be strategically enhanced through operational improvements, expansion, or financial restructuring.

1. Scalability

Scalability is a key consideration for private equity firms when evaluating a potential acquisition. Scalability refers to the company's ability to grow revenue and profits without a proportional increase in costs. Companies that can scale efficiently are highly attractive because they offer the potential for rapid growth and high returns on investment.

Private equity firms look for businesses that have the infrastructure, processes, and market position to support significant growth. This might include businesses with a strong customer base, proven sales processes, and the ability to expand into new regions or product categories without requiring substantial capital investment.

Examples of scalable businesses include:

- Technology companies with low incremental costs for serving additional customers

- Franchises or multi-location businesses that can replicate their business model in new markets

- Manufacturing companies with the capacity to increase production without a significant increase in fixed costs

2. Strategic Fit

Private equity firms also evaluate how well a potential acquisition fits within their overall portfolio or investment thesis. Many PE firms specialize in specific industries or sectors, and they look for companies that complement their existing holdings or align with their expertise. A company that fits strategically with the PE firm's other investments can offer synergies, such as shared resources, cost efficiencies, or cross-selling opportunities.

In some cases, a private equity firm may be pursuing a broader strategic initiative, such as building a platform company or executing a roll-up strategy. In these cases, the target company may serve as the foundation for future acquisitions, allowing the PE firm to create a larger, more competitive entity over time.

A strategic fit may be evaluated based on factors such as:

- The target company's alignment with the PE firm's investment strategy or sector focus

- Opportunities to create synergies with other companies in the PE firm's portfolio

- The potential for the target company to serve as a platform for future acquisitions

3. Barriers to Entry

Companies with strong barriers to entry are highly attractive to private equity firms. Barriers to entry make it difficult for new competitors to enter the market, which protects the company's market share and pricing power. These barriers can take many forms, including proprietary technology, regulatory approvals, customer relationships, or high capital requirements.

PE firms are particularly interested in companies that have built defensible positions within their market. These businesses are less vulnerable to competitive pressures and are more likely to sustain long-term growth. Additionally, companies with high barriers to entry may command premium valuations, as they offer a more stable and predictable revenue stream.

Examples of barriers to entry include:

- Patented technology or proprietary processes that competitors cannot easily replicate

- Regulatory approvals or certifications that are difficult to obtain

- Long-term contracts or exclusive relationships with key customers

4. Operational Efficiency

Operational efficiency is another critical factor in a company's growth potential and strategic value. Private equity firms often target companies that are operationally inefficient because they see opportunities to improve margins and create value through cost reductions, process improvements, or better resource allocation.

Companies with strong operational efficiency are able to maximize profitability and cash flow, which in turn provides the capital needed to fund growth initiatives. PE firms look for businesses that can improve their operations through better supply chain management, automation, or leaner production processes.

Some indicators of operational efficiency include:

- High margins relative to industry peers

- Low overhead costs as a percentage of revenue

- Efficient use of capital and strong return on investment (ROI)

Signs Your Company
May be a Target

Given the factors that drive private equity interest, there are several signs that indicate a company may be a target for acquisition. If a company exhibits these characteristics, it is likely to attract attention from PE firms, and business owners and managers should be prepared for potential inquiries or offers.

1. Consistent Profitability and Strong Cash Flow

Private equity firms are drawn to companies that generate consistent profitability and strong cash flow. These companies offer a stable foundation for growth, and their predictable cash flow makes them attractive for leveraged buyouts (LBOs), where the company's future earnings are used to service the debt incurred in the acquisition.

If your company consistently delivers strong financial results, with healthy margins and reliable cash flow, it is likely to be on the radar of PE firms looking for acquisition opportunities.

2. Strong Market Position

Companies with a strong market position, particularly in niche markets or fragmented industries, are attractive targets for private equity. If your company is a market leader or has a unique competitive advantage, PE firms may see an opportunity to build on that position through additional investment or strategic acquisitions.

Signs that your company has a strong market position include:

- High market share relative to competitors

- Strong brand recognition and customer loyalty

- Competitive advantages that are difficult for others to replicate

3. Ownership Transition or Succession Planning

If your company is undergoing or preparing for an ownership transition, such as a founder's retirement or a generational handover in a family business, it may attract the attention of private equity firms. PE firms are often interested in companies that require new leadership and are willing to step in to provide both capital and management expertise during the transition.

4. Growth Potential Without Access to Capital

If your company has significant growth potential but lacks the capital to execute on its expansion plans, you may be a target for private equity acquisition. PE firms specialize in providing the financial resources and strategic guidance needed to scale a business, making them a natural partner for companies that are poised for growth but constrained by capital limitations.

5. Industry Trends Favorable to Consolidation

If your company operates in an industry that is undergoing consolidation, it may be a target for private equity firms looking to build a larger, more competitive entity through acquisitions. PE firms often pursue roll-up strategies in fragmented industries, and your company could be a valuable piece of the puzzle in creating a market leader.

Workshop Activities

Analyze Strategic vs. Financial Buyers

Objective: Understand the difference between strategic and financial buyers and why a private equity firm may view a company differently than a strategic acquirer.

Instructions:

- Seek examples of acquisitions made by both strategic buyers (e.g., companies in the same or related industry) and financial buyers (e.g., private equity firms).

- Analyze the differences in:

  » How each buyer views value creation

  » The types of companies each buyer targets

  » What each buyer expects post-acquisition (e.g., synergies for strategic buyers, financial returns for PE Review how these differences impact the way companies present themselves as acquisition targets to strategic vs. financial buyers.

- **Output:** A comparison of how strategic and financial buyers approach acquisitions, including how value is measured differently.

- **Actionable Takeaway:** You will gain a clear understanding of how private equity firms (financial buyers) assess acquisitions compared to strategic buyers, enabling them to tailor strategies depending on the type of buyer.

Conclusion

Private equity acquisitions are driven by a range of factors, from the need for capital to fund growth to the potential for operational improvements and strategic synergies. Companies that exhibit strong growth potential, operational efficiency, and defensible market positions are particularly attractive to PE firms. By understanding the triggers for private equity interest, business owners and managers can better position themselves for acquisition or prepare to capitalize on the opportunities that arise when PE firms come knocking. Whether your company is actively seeking investment or simply wants to be prepared for potential inquiries, recognizing the signs of PE interest and understanding the factors that drive it will help you navigate the process with confidence.

MANAGING THE TRANSITION

Once a private equity firm acquires a company, the work truly begins. The transition period is where theory turns into practice, and this phase can make or break the long-term success of the acquisition. For the employees, management, and leadership of the acquired company, the first 100 days after the deal closes are critical. It's a time of uncertainty, but also opportunity. Expectations are high, and the pace of change can be swift. Knowing what to expect and how to navigate this transitional period will help all parties involved adapt quickly, align with new ownership, and set the company on a path for future growth and success.

In this section, we will explore how to manage the critical post-acquisition period. From understanding the changes in leadership and governance to establishing open communication channels with the new owners, the following chapters will provide a roadmap for navigating this often challenging but pivotal phase. The goal is to ensure that all stakeholders, from top leadership to frontline employees, are aligned with the private equity firm's objectives and positioned for long-term success.

CHAPTER 4

The First 100 Days Post-Acquisition

"

The first 100 days set the stage for long-term success—focus on clear communication, strategic action, and leadership alignment.

"

The first 100 days following a private equity acquisition are crucial for laying the groundwork for future success. This period typically involves significant changes in leadership, strategy, and operations. Managing these changes effectively is vital for the company's future trajectory. While the transition might be unsettling for employees, it also opens up opportunities for new goals and growth initiatives. This chapter discusses the typical changes post-acquisition, how to navigate shifts in leadership and governance, and maintaining open communication with new owners to ensure a smooth transition and position the company for success.

Transition Timelines:
What to Expect

Once the ink is dry on the acquisition, the real work begins. The first 100 days can be characterized as a time of assessment, rapid change, and immediate action. Private equity firms typically have a clear vision for how they want the company to evolve, and this vision often involves a blend of strategic, operational, and financial changes. Here's what to expect during this time:

1. Assessment Phase (Days 1-30):

In the first few weeks, the private equity firm will conduct a more in-depth evaluation of the company. Although they've already completed extensive due diligence during the acquisition process, the post-close assessment provides them with real-time data on the company's operations, financials, and personnel. This phase often involves:

- Meeting with department heads to gain insights into day-to-day operations

- Reviewing financial statements and identifying discrepancies or areas for improvement

- Assessing existing systems and technologies to determine what needs upgrading or replacement

- Understanding the company culture and employee morale

For employees, this phase can feel like a whirlwind of meetings and audits. The PE firm will want to gather as much information as possible to make informed decisions about the next steps. During this time, it's crucial for the management team to remain open, cooperative, and proactive in sharing information and insights.

2. Strategic Realignment (Days 30-60):

Once the assessment phase is complete, the private equity firm will begin realigning the company's strategy to fit its goals for value creation. This phase often involves a shift in priorities, with an emphasis on:

- Streamlining operations and cutting unnecessary costs
- Identifying areas for immediate revenue growth, such as expanding product lincs, entering new markets, or increasing pricing
- Implementing quick-win initiatives that can show progress early on, such as renegotiating supplier contracts or optimizing the sales funnel

During this phase, some strategic pivots may occur, and employees should expect to see a clear outline of new business objectives. The PE firm will work closely with the management team to ensure that these initiatives are understood and acted upon.

3. Implementation and Quick Wins (Days 60-100):

The last phase of the first 100 days is where the initial changes are fully implemented. The focus during this period is on execution, delivering quick wins, and building momentum for the long-term changes to come. The private equity firm will expect to see tangible results during this phase, such as:

- Increased cash flow from operational improvements
- Cost savings from streamlining processes or cutting underperforming assets

- Early indicators of revenue growth from new sales or marketing strategies

While this period can be intense, it is also a time to show the new owners what the company can achieve. Employees and managers should focus on hitting short-term targets, delivering early wins, and positioning the company for sustained success.

Transition Services Agreements (TSAs): Structure for Success

A **Transition Services Agreement (TSA)** is a contractual agreement between the buyer and seller, typically implemented when the seller continues to provide critical services to the buyer for a defined period post-acquisition. TSAs help ensure operational continuity while the acquiring company transitions fully to its new structure.

Why TSAs Matter

TSAs are particularly important when a company is acquired by private equity, as many functions—such as IT, HR, or finance—may still rely on the seller's systems and infrastructure. Properly structuring a TSA is critical to ensuring that both parties understand their obligations, minimizing disruptions and avoiding delays during the transition.

Best Practices for Structuring a TSA
1. Define Clear Scope of Services

A successful TSA starts with a well-defined scope. Both the buyer and seller must clearly understand which services are being provided, their expected quality, and any specific deliverables required. This could include IT support, payroll management, data migration, or accounting functions.

2. Set Realistic Timelines

TSAs are typically temporary and designed to last between 3 to 12 months. It's critical to establish a realistic timeline for the transition and ensure that all milestones are achievable within the TSA term. The agreement should include a plan for the buyer to take over or replace the services being provided by the seller, and this timeline should include provisions for an extension if unforeseen issues arise.

3. Identify Key Deliverables

Break down the key deliverables that need to be met within the agreed-upon TSA timeline. Whether it's the completion of IT systems migration, financial reporting, or the transition of employee benefits systems, these deliverables should be clearly laid out with target dates for completion.

4. Assign Responsibilities and Points of Contact

Ensure that both the buyer and seller have clearly defined points of contact for managing the TSA. These individuals should be responsible for overseeing the transition, troubleshooting issues, and communicating progress. This helps avoid confusion and ensures accountability on both sides.

5. Establish Service Level Agreements (SLAs)

TSAs should include SLAs to ensure that the quality and availability of services remain consistent throughout the transition. SLAs set expectations for performance metrics, response times, and issue resolution, ensuring that both parties are held to a professional standard.

6. Plan for Contingencies and Risks

Identify potential risks that could disrupt the transition process, such as technical difficulties or resource constraints, and include contingency plans in the TSA. This could involve having backup service providers in place or adding flexibility to the timeline for specific services.

7. Ensure Regular Reviews and Communication

Set up regular review meetings with the seller to assess progress on key deliverables and make adjustments if necessary. Frequent communication helps ensure that both parties are aligned and that any issues can be addressed before they escalate.

Avoiding TSA Term Overruns

One of the biggest risks associated with TSAs is that the transition takes longer than expected, leading to costly TSA term extensions. To avoid running over the TSA term:

- **Start the transition early:** Begin migrating systems, processes, and services as soon as possible after the acquisition closes.

- **Monitor progress rigorously:** Set clear deadlines and hold regular status meetings to ensure that milestones are being met.

- **Be proactive about issue resolution:** Quickly address any challenges that arise during the transition to avoid delays that could extend the TSA term.

By structuring your TSA thoughtfully and focusing on achieving key milestones, you can avoid delays and ensure a smooth handoff of services from the seller to the buyer.

Changes in Leadership and Governance

One of the most immediate and visible changes post-acquisition is likely to occur at the leadership and governance level. Private equity firms often make swift decisions when it comes to the executive team, especially if they believe that current leadership is not aligned with their goals or capable of executing their strategy.

Here's what to expect in terms of leadership changes:

1. New Executive Appointments:

PE firms frequently appoint new executives—particularly a new CEO, CFO, or COO—who are experienced in managing businesses under private equity ownership. These new leaders are brought in to drive the PE firm's agenda and ensure that the company delivers on its growth and profitability goals. The management team may also be supplemented with functional experts in areas like sales, marketing, or operations to bolster the company's capabilities.

For the existing management team, this transition can be both challenging and an opportunity for growth. Some leaders may exit the company voluntarily or as part of the buyout, while others may be invited to stay and work alongside the new leadership. In many cases, private equity firms prefer to retain senior leaders who have valuable institutional knowledge but pair them with new executives who bring fresh perspectives and a track record of success.

2. Changes to the Board of Directors:

The governance structure of the company will also change. After a PE acquisition, the private equity firm typically takes control of the board of directors, appointing their own representatives to oversee the company's strategic direction. This means that the board will shift from representing the interests of the previous owners or shareholders to focusing exclusively on the goals of the PE firm.

The new board will have a more hands-on role than traditional corporate boards, meeting frequently and providing direct input on major decisions. PE firms expect regular updates on performance, and they will hold the management team accountable for delivering results. This shift in governance can be an adjustment for companies that were previously privately owned or operated with a more decentralized board.

3. Key Talent Retention and Realignment:

In many cases, private equity firms will introduce new incentive structures to retain top talent and ensure alignment with the company's new goals. This often takes the form of performance-based compensation packages, such as equity or stock options, that are tied to the company's success.

For employees, these incentives can be highly motivating, as they provide a direct stake in the company's future performance. However, they also raise the stakes, as employees are expected to meet ambitious performance targets to realize these rewards.

In some cases, the PE firm may also realign roles and responsibilities within the organization. This might involve promoting high-potential employees into leadership roles or restructuring departments to better align with the company's new strategic priorities.

Establishing Communication Channels with New Owners

Effective communication between the management team and the new owners is crucial during the first 100 days post-acquisition. Private equity firms rely on timely and accurate information to make informed decisions and adjust their strategies as needed. Therefore, establishing open, transparent communication channels is one of the top priorities in the early days of the transition.

Here are some key considerations for establishing these communication channels:

1. Regular Meetings and Reporting Structures:

One of the first steps in establishing communication with the new owners is to set up a regular cadence of meetings and reporting. This typically includes weekly or bi-weekly meetings with the PE firm's representatives, where the management team provides updates on key performance metrics, progress on strategic initiatives, and any challenges or roadblocks.

The PE firm will also expect detailed financial and operational reports that provide insight into the company's performance. These reports should be transparent and data-driven, with a focus on measurable results. For the management team, this may require setting up new reporting systems or upgrading existing ones to ensure that the right data is being tracked and communicated.

2. Aligning on Key Metrics and Goals:

Private equity firms are highly metrics-driven, and they expect the management team to focus on the key performance indicators (KPIs) that matter most for value creation. Early in the transition, it's essential to align with the PE firm on what these metrics are and how they will be measured. Common KPIs include revenue growth, EBITDA margins, cash flow, customer acquisition costs, and return on investment (ROI).

By establishing a shared understanding of the key metrics, the management team can focus their efforts on what matters most to the PE firm. This alignment also helps to ensure that everyone is working toward the same goals, reducing confusion or misalignment during the transition.

3. Clear and Consistent Communication with Employees:

In addition to communicating with the new owners, it's equally important to establish clear communication channels with the broader employee base. The first 100 days can be a time of uncertainty for employees, and without proper communication, rumors and anxiety can spread quickly.

The management team should provide regular updates to employees about the progress of the transition, the company's new strategic direction, and any changes that may affect their roles. Transparency is key—employees should feel informed and confident that leadership is guiding the company through the transition effectively.

Town hall meetings, internal newsletters, and one-on-one check-ins are all effective tools for keeping employees engaged and informed during this period. The more the management team can communicate a sense of stability and purpose, the smoother the transition will be.

4. Building Trust with the New Owners:

Finally, building trust with the new owners is essential for a successful transition. Private equity firms place a high value on management teams that can execute their vision effectively, and the first 100 days are a time to prove that you can deliver.

Trust is built through transparency, accountability, and results. By keeping the lines of communication open, providing honest updates, and delivering on the early goals set by the PE firm, the management team can establish a strong working relationship with the new owners. This trust will be critical as the company moves beyond the transition phase and into its next chapter of growth.

Workshop Activities

Objective: Create a comprehensive transition plan for the first 100 days after a private equity acquisition, focusing on key priorities, timelines, and milestones.

Instructions:

- Create a 100-day transition plan for a fictional company that has just been acquired by a private equity firm.

- Consider the following areas:
  - » Immediate operational changes
  - » Leadership transitions and new governance structures
  - » Employee communication and engagement
  - » Financial goals (e.g., improving cash flow, cost-cutting)
  - » Quick wins and long-term goals
- Create a timeline with key milestones for the first 100 days, ensuring the plan is realistic and actionable.

Output: Review your 100-day transition plan, know why you prioritized certain tasks and how your plan will help ensure a smooth post-acquisition transition.

Actionable Takeaway: You will understand how to prioritize activities during the first 100 days post-acquisition and build realistic transition plans that balance immediate needs with long-term strategy.

Conclusion

The first 100 days post-acquisition are a whirlwind of assessment, change, and action. For both the management team and employees, it's a time to adapt to new leadership, new goals, and new expectations. Understanding what to expect during this period—whether it's changes in governance, leadership, or communication structures—can help smooth the transition and set the stage for long-term success. Private equity firms expect results, and the first

100 days are a proving ground for whether the company can deliver on the promises made during the acquisition. By managing the transition effectively, establishing strong communication channels with the new owners, and focusing on quick wins, the management team can ensure that the company is well-positioned for the future.

CHAPTER 5

Navigating Cultural Shifts

‟

Building bridges between old and new cultures is the key to unlocking innovation, engagement, and a thriving post-acquisition company.

„

One of the most challenging aspects of a private equity acquisition is managing the cultural shifts that inevitably occur when new ownership steps in. Culture is the backbone of any organization, shaping how employees interact, make decisions, and execute on strategy. When a private equity firm acquires a company, it often brings with it a new set of goals, values, and expectations. Navigating these changes while maintaining the core strengths of the company's legacy culture is essential for long-term success.

In this chapter, we will explore how to understand and align with the private equity firm's goals and values, the delicate task of balancing the company's existing culture with new demands, and how to build bridges between the existing team and new leadership. The ability to navigate these cultural shifts will not only help the company thrive but also create a more cohesive and productive working environment.

Understanding the PE Firm's

Goals and Values

At the heart of any successful transition is a deep understanding of what the private equity firm aims to achieve. Unlike traditional owners, private equity firms often have a clear, time-bound vision for how they want the company to perform and evolve. This vision is typically rooted in creating significant financial returns within a specific time frame, usually between three and seven years. Understanding the goals and values of the PE firm is critical in aligning the company's culture with its new direction.

1. Financial Performance as a Priority

Private equity firms are fundamentally focused on delivering financial returns for their investors. This means that the primary goal of the acquisition is to increase the value of the company and eventually sell it for a profit. Financial performance is the driving force behind most decisions, and this can sometimes feel at odds with a company's existing culture, especially if it has been more focused on long-term growth, innovation, or customer-centric values.

Understanding this focus on financial performance is key. It doesn't mean that the company's legacy values, such as employee well-being or customer satisfaction, will be discarded, but it does mean that every initiative and decision will be evaluated through the lens of how it impacts profitability and growth. Employees and management need to recognize that this shift in priorities is not just a change in focus but a fundamental part of the PE firm's operating model.

2. Efficiency and Operational Improvement

PE firms are often experts in streamlining operations and improving efficiency. They come into acquisitions with a strong emphasis on optimizing processes, cutting unnecessary costs, and driving higher margins. This can sometimes feel disruptive to employees, particularly in companies where the culture has been more relaxed or focused on other goals, like innovation or employee development.

Recognizing that efficiency is a core value of most private equity firms can help employees understand why changes are being made. This shift towards operational improvement is not about undermining the company's past achievements, but rather about ensuring that the business can operate more effectively and competitively in the future.

3. Accountability and Data-Driven Decision Making

Another key value of private equity firms is a strong emphasis on accountability and performance measurement. PE firms tend to rely heavily on data to make decisions, and they expect the companies they acquire to adopt the same approach. This means that KPIs (key performance indicators) and metrics will play a larger role in how success is defined, and employees at all levels will be held accountable for meeting these targets.

The culture of accountability can feel like a significant shift for employees who are used to more flexibility or autonomy in their roles. However, embracing this focus on measurable outcomes can ultimately lead to greater clarity, transparency, and fairness in how performance is evaluated across the organization.

4. Short-Term vs. Long-Term Focus

One of the most significant cultural shifts in a private equity acquisition is the balance between short-term and long-term goals. PE firms typically operate with a shorter time horizon than traditional owners, as they aim to increase the company's value quickly and prepare for an eventual exit. This can create pressure to prioritize short-term gains, such as improving quarterly financial performance or cutting costs, over long-term investments in innovation, talent development, or new markets.

While this focus on short-term results can feel unsettling, it's important to remember that the PE firm's goal is to build a stronger, more competitive company. The challenge for employees and management is to align with the firm's immediate objectives while finding ways to preserve the company's long-term vision and core strengths.

Balancing Legacy Culture with New Demands

When a private equity firm acquires a company, it often brings new expectations that can conflict with the company's existing culture. Managing this tension between the legacy culture and the new demands of the PE firm is a delicate balancing act, but it's crucial for maintaining employee morale and ensuring that the company doesn't lose what made it successful in the first place.

1. Identify the Core Elements of Legacy Culture

The first step in balancing legacy culture with new demands is to identify the core elements of the company's existing culture that have contributed to its success. Every company has certain cultural strengths that drive performance, whether it's a commitment to innovation, a customer-centric approach, or a strong sense of teamwork and collaboration.

It's important for leadership to acknowledge and protect these cultural strengths, even as the company adapts to new ownership. By identifying and preserving the elements of the legacy culture that have contributed to the company's growth and success, the management team can help ensure that employees feel valued and that the company doesn't lose its identity in the transition.

2. Aligning Culture with the New Strategic Priorities

While it's important to preserve the core elements of the company's legacy culture, it's equally important to align the culture with the private equity firm's new strategic priorities. This requires a thoughtful approach to change management, where leadership helps employees understand why certain cultural shifts are necessary and how they fit into the broader strategy.

For example, if the PE firm is focused on improving operational efficiency, leadership may need to introduce new processes or technologies that streamline work. However, these changes should be framed in a way that aligns with the company's existing values.

If teamwork and collaboration are core elements of the company's culture, for instance, the new processes should be introduced in a way that enhances collaboration, rather than undermining it.

The goal is to create a culture that is flexible enough to adapt to new demands but strong enough to retain the values that made the company successful in the first place.

3. Communicating the Importance of Cultural Evolution

One of the biggest challenges in navigating cultural shifts is overcoming resistance to change. Employees who are deeply invested in the company's legacy culture may be wary of the changes that come with new ownership. To address this, leadership must communicate the importance of cultural evolution and how it benefits the company and its employees in the long run.

Employees need to understand that the private equity firm's goals are not about erasing the company's history or identity but about building on its strengths and ensuring its long-term success. By framing cultural shifts as part of the company's growth and evolution, rather than a complete overhaul, leadership can help ease the transition and reduce resistance.

4. Creating a Culture of Adaptability

One of the most valuable cultural traits a company can develop in the wake of a private equity acquisition is adaptability. In today's fast-paced business environment, companies that are able to adapt quickly to new market conditions, technologies, and customer demands are the ones that thrive. Private equity firms often push for rapid changes, and the more adaptable the company's culture is, the easier it will be to navigate these shifts.

Fostering a culture of adaptability means encouraging employees to embrace change rather than fear it. This can be done through training programs that focus on developing new skills, open communication about the reasons behind changes, and a strong emphasis on continuous improvement.

How to Build Bridges Between
Existing Teams and New Leadership

The success of a private equity acquisition often depends on how well the existing team and the new leadership can work together. Building bridges between these groups is essential for ensuring that the company can move forward with a united vision and shared goals.

1. Foster Open Communication and Transparency

The first step in building bridges between existing teams and new leadership is to establish open lines of communication. In the early days of the transition, it's common for employees to feel uncertain about the new leadership's goals and expectations. This uncertainty can lead to confusion, misalignment, and even distrust.

New leadership should make an effort to communicate openly and transparently with the existing team. This means sharing the company's new strategic direction, explaining the reasons behind any changes, and addressing any concerns or questions employees may have. By fostering a culture of transparency, new leadership can build trust and create a more collaborative environment.

2. Respect the Expertise and Institutional Knowledge of Existing Teams

One of the biggest mistakes new leadership can make during a private equity acquisition is to disregard the expertise and institutional knowledge of the existing team. Employees who have been with the company for years, or even decades, have a deep understanding of its operations, customers, and culture. Their insights are invaluable in helping the new leadership team navigate the company's unique challenges and opportunities.

New leadership should make an effort to engage with the existing team, listen to their perspectives, and involve them in decision-making processes. By showing respect for the team's expertise and institutional knowledge, new leadership can build stronger relationships and ensure a smoother transition.

3. Integrate New Leadership with Existing Team Dynamics

While it's important for new leadership to bring fresh perspectives and ideas, it's equally important to integrate them into the existing team dynamics. This requires a delicate balance between introducing new leadership styles and respecting the company's established ways of working.

One way to do this is through team-building activities that allow new leaders to connect with existing employees on a more personal level. By fostering positive relationships outside of formal meetings and work environments, new leadership can build trust and rapport with the team.

4. Establish Clear Roles and Responsibilities

One of the most common sources of tension between existing teams and new leadership is a lack of clarity around roles and responsibilities. When new leaders are brought in, there can be uncertainty about who is responsible for what, leading to confusion and frustration.

To avoid this, it's essential to establish clear roles and responsibilities from the outset. This includes defining the scope of authority for new leaders, outlining the decision-making process, and ensuring that all employees understand how their roles fit into the company's new strategic direction. By providing clarity, leadership can reduce friction and create a more cohesive working environment.

5. Focus on Shared Goals and Collaboration

Finally, building bridges between existing teams and new leadership requires a focus on shared goals and collaboration. It's important to emphasize that both groups are working toward the same objective: the success of the company. By fostering a sense of shared purpose, leadership can unite the team and create a more collaborative, productive working environment.

Encouraging cross-functional collaboration, where existing teams and new leaders work together on strategic initiatives, can help break down silos and build stronger relationships. This collaborative approach not only strengthens the company's culture but also ensures that the best ideas and solutions are brought to the table.

Workshop Activities

Building Bridges Between Teams and New Leadership

Objective: Design a plan to foster collaboration and trust between existing teams and new leadership.

Instructions:

- Develop a scenario where a company's existing teams feel disconnected from the new leadership introduced by the PE firm.

- Create a plan to build bridges between the two sides, focusing on:

  » Identifying trust-building activities (e.g., team-building events, cross-functional meetings, town halls).

  » Establishing open communication channels between leadership and teams (e.g., regular updates, open Q&A sessions).

  » Creating opportunities for collaborative decision-making, ensuring that legacy employees feel valued and heard.

> » Providing transparency around decision-making and the goals of the new leadership team.

- Create a detailed plan outlining specific actions that leadership can take to foster collaboration and improve trust.

Output: A bridge-building plan designed to foster trust and collaboration between existing teams and new leadership, with specific activities and timelines.

Actionable Takeaway: You will learn how to facilitate collaboration and trust-building between teams and new leadership, ensuring smoother cultural transitions post-acquisition.

Conclusion

Navigating cultural shifts is one of the most challenging aspects of a private equity acquisition, but it's also one of the most important. By understanding the goals and values of the private equity firm, balancing the legacy culture with new demands, and building bridges between existing teams and new leadership, companies can successfully manage the transition and emerge stronger on the other side. Cultural change doesn't happen overnight, but with thoughtful planning, clear communication, and a commitment to preserving the company's core strengths, it is possible to create a culture that is both adaptable and aligned with the company's new direction.

CHAPTER 6

Re-Defining Roles And Responsibilities

"

Embrace change as an opportunity to redefine roles, empower your team, and drive your organization forward with confidence.

"

One of the most profound changes that occur following a private equity (PE) acquisition is the redefinition of roles and responsibilities within the company. For both management and employees, these changes can feel disorienting, but they are a necessary part of aligning the business with the goals of the new ownership. As private equity firms focus on maximizing efficiency, streamlining operations, and driving growth, the organizational structure is often adjusted to meet these new priorities.

This chapter will explore the key aspects of re-defining roles and responsibilities post-acquisition, including how to adjust to new reporting structures, manage relationships with PE owners, and handle the inevitable uncertainty and resistance to change that accompanies such transitions.

Adjusting to New Reporting Structures

One of the immediate impacts of a PE acquisition is the introduction of new reporting structures. Private equity firms are highly data-driven, and they rely on transparent, efficient reporting mechanisms to monitor progress, assess performance, and make strategic decisions. For employees and management, this often means adapting to new expectations around accountability, performance metrics, and the flow of information within the company.

1. The Shift from Informal to Formal Reporting

In many privately owned or family-run businesses, reporting structures tend to be more informal. Decisions might be made through direct conversations, and performance assessments may focus more on qualitative feedback than on detailed metrics. Post-acquisition, however, this is likely to change. PE firms require rigorous reporting systems that provide quantifiable, real-time insights into the company's financial health, operational efficiency, and overall performance.

Key elements of this shift include:

- **Standardized Reporting Systems:** Private equity firms often implement standardized reporting tools and dashboards that track key performance indicators (KPIs) across all departments. This enables the PE firm to quickly assess how each part of the business is performing and identify areas that require attention.

- **Increased Frequency of Reporting:** Unlike the quarterly or annual reports that may have been sufficient under previous ownership, PE firms typically require more frequent updates—often monthly, bi-weekly, or even weekly. This ensures that they have a clear, up-to-date picture of the company's trajectory at all times.

- **Greater Emphasis on Data and Metrics:** In the PE environment, decisions are heavily influenced by data. This means that reporting will focus on hard metrics such as revenue growth, cash flow, cost margins, productivity rates, and customer acquisition metrics. For many employees, especially those used to more qualitative performance assessments, this shift can require significant adjustment.

2. Adapting to Layered Reporting Hierarchies

Another major adjustment in post-acquisition reporting structures is the introduction of layered hierarchies. PE firms typically install a new governance model, which often involves a board of directors or oversight committee composed of representatives from the private equity firm, along with any external advisors brought in to guide strategy. This structure creates additional layers of accountability and reporting between the company's management team and the ultimate owners.

This multi-layered reporting system may include:

- **Direct Reporting to the PE Firm:** Senior executives, such as the CEO and CFO, will often report directly to the PE firm's managing directors or partners. These reporting relationships will focus on high-level strategic initiatives, financial performance, and key operational outcomes.

- **Internal Reporting for Day-to-Day Operations:** Mid-level managers and department heads will be tasked with reporting to the company's senior executives. This creates a more structured chain of command, where each layer of the business is accountable to the layer above it, ensuring that information flows smoothly from the operational level to the executive level and then on to the PE owners.

- **Board-Level Reporting:** The company's CEO and senior leadership will typically present reports to the PE-appointed board of directors on a regular basis. These presentations focus on major strategic milestones, financial results, and any potential risks or challenges the company is facing. The board, in turn, will provide guidance and approval on key decisions.

3. Ensuring Alignment with PE Expectations

One of the most important aspects of adjusting to new reporting structures is ensuring alignment with the PE firm's expectations. Private equity firms are results-oriented, and they expect the management team to meet clearly defined targets, often within tight timelines. This requires not only accurate reporting but also a shared understanding of the goals and performance metrics that the PE firm values most.

Steps to ensure alignment include:

- **Clear Communication of KPIs:** Management must ensure that all employees understand the key metrics that the PE firm is tracking. This involves not only defining these KPIs but also explaining why they are important and how they contribute to the company's overall success.

- **Regular Performance Reviews:** In a PE-backed company, performance reviews will likely be conducted more frequently and will be more data-driven than before.

Managers need to schedule regular check-ins with their teams to review progress, address any performance gaps, and ensure that everyone is aligned with the company's strategic goals.

- **Continuous Feedback Loops:** It's critical to establish feedback loops that allow for ongoing communication between employees, managers, and the PE firm. This ensures that any issues are identified and addressed early, before they become larger problems.

Managing Relationships with the PE Owners

Managing relationships with the private equity owners is an essential component of navigating a successful transition. PE owners play a hands-on role in overseeing the company's performance and guiding its strategic direction, and they expect the management team to execute on their vision with precision and speed. Building and maintaining a strong, productive relationship with the PE firm is key to ensuring that the company remains on track to achieve its goals.

1. Understanding the Role of the PE Firm

One of the first steps in managing relationships with the PE owners is understanding their role in the company. Private equity firms are not passive investors—they are actively involved in shaping the company's strategy, driving operational improvements, and monitoring financial performance. They often bring in their own industry experts, advisors, or consultants to help implement best practices and optimize processes.

The PE firm's involvement typically includes:

- **Strategic Oversight:** The PE firm will work closely with the company's executive team to define the strategic direction of the business. This includes setting growth targets, identifying opportunities for expansion, and ensuring that the company is positioned for a successful exit in the future.

- **Financial Control:** Private equity owners are deeply focused on financial performance, and they will expect the management team to meet or exceed financial targets. This often involves close scrutiny of the company's budget, cost structure, and cash flow management.

- **Operational Guidance:** Many PE firms bring operational expertise to the table, helping the company implement leaner, more efficient processes. This can range from improving supply chain management to optimizing production schedules or reducing overhead costs.

2. Building Trust with the PE Firm

Trust is a critical component of any successful relationship, and this is especially true when working with private equity owners. Building trust requires transparency, accountability, and consistent delivery of results. The PE firm needs to have confidence in the management team's ability to execute on its vision and drive the business forward.

Key ways to build trust include:

- **Open and Honest Communication:** One of the most effective ways to build trust with the PE firm is through open and honest communication. Management should provide regular updates on the company's performance, including both successes and challenges. If issues arise, it's better to address them head-on rather than trying to hide them.

- **Delivering on Promises:** PE firms value execution, and they expect the management team to deliver on the goals and targets that have been set. Meeting or exceeding performance targets consistently will help build confidence and strengthen the relationship with the PE firm.

- **Proactive Problem-Solving:** In a private equity-backed company, challenges are inevitable. What sets strong management teams apart is their ability to proactively identify problems and implement solutions before they escalate. This demonstrates to the PE firm that the team is capable of managing the business effectively and can handle any obstacles that come their way.

3. Navigating Differences in Approach

It's not uncommon for differences in approach to arise between the management team and the PE owners, especially when it comes to strategic priorities or operational decisions. PE firms may push for faster growth, more aggressive cost-cutting measures, or changes in the company's product or service offerings, while the management team may have a different perspective based on its deeper knowledge of the company and its market.

To navigate these differences:

- **Seek to Understand the PE Firm's Perspective:** PE firms often have a broader industry perspective, and they bring valuable insights from their experience with other portfolio companies. Management should take the time to understand the rationale behind the PE firm's recommendations and consider how these ideas could benefit the company.

- **Present Data-Backed Arguments:** When disagreements arise, it's important for the management team to present data-backed arguments for their position. PE firms rely on data to make decisions, and providing clear, quantitative evidence can help bridge the gap between different perspectives.

- **Compromise and Collaboration:** Successful relationships between management and PE owners require compromise and collaboration. Both sides should be willing to adjust their approach in order to find a solution that aligns with the company's overall goals. By fostering a culture of collaboration, management can ensure that the company is able to navigate challenges and seize opportunities effectively.

Dealing with Uncertainty and Resistance to Change

Change is an inevitable part of any private equity acquisition, and with change often comes uncertainty and resistance. Employees at all levels may feel anxious about the future, unsure of what the new ownership will mean for their roles, their responsibilities, and their long-term prospects with the company. Managing this uncertainty and overcoming resistance to change is one of the biggest challenges that leaders face during the transition.

1. Recognizing the Sources of Uncertainty

Uncertainty can stem from a variety of factors, including changes in leadership, shifts in strategic direction, and concerns about job security. For employees who have been with the company for a long time, the acquisition may feel like a disruption to the status quo, and they may worry about how their roles will be affected.

Common sources of uncertainty include:

- **Job Security:** Employees may fear layoffs or restructuring, especially if the PE firm has a reputation for making significant changes to streamline operations.

- **Role Changes:** As roles and responsibilities are redefined, employees may feel uncertain about how their position will evolve. Will they have new duties? Will they report to a different manager? These questions can create anxiety.

- **Cultural Shifts:** Changes in the company's culture can also contribute to uncertainty. If the PE firm's goals and values differ from the company's legacy culture, employees may worry that the environment they've grown accustomed to will disappear.

2. Communicating with Empathy and Clarity

One of the most effective ways to address uncertainty is through clear, empathetic communication. Leadership should make a concerted effort to provide employees with regular updates on the transition process, explain the reasons behind any changes, and offer reassurance about the company's future.

Key strategies for communicating during times of uncertainty:

- **Provide Regular Updates:** Employees should be kept informed about key developments in the acquisition process and any changes that are being implemented. Regular town hall meetings, email updates, or internal newsletters can help keep employees in the loop and reduce speculation.

- **Be Transparent About Changes:** If changes are being made to roles or responsibilities, it's important to be transparent about why these changes are necessary and how they will benefit the company in the long run. Employees are more likely to accept changes if they understand the rationale behind them.

- **Acknowledge Employee Concerns:** Leadership should acknowledge that uncertainty and anxiety are natural responses to change. By listening to employee concerns and offering support, leaders can help ease the transition and create a more positive work environment.

3. Overcoming Resistance to Change

Resistance to change is a common challenge in any organizational transition, and private equity acquisitions are no exception. Employees who are comfortable with the way things have always been may resist new processes, reporting structures, or performance expectations. Overcoming this resistance requires a combination of strong leadership, clear communication, and a focus on the long-term benefits of the changes.

Steps to overcome resistance to change:

- **Involve Employees in the Process:** One of the most effective ways to reduce resistance is to involve employees in the change process. By soliciting their input and involving them in decision-making, leadership can help employees feel more invested in the company's future.

- **Provide Training and Support:** Employees may resist change simply because they feel unprepared for new roles or responsibilities. Offering training programs, mentorship, and support can help employees develop the skills they need to succeed in the new environment.

- **Highlight the Benefits of Change:** Leadership should communicate the benefits of the changes being implemented, both for the company and for employees themselves. Whether it's increased efficiency, new growth opportunities, or improved job security, employees are more likely to embrace change if they see how it will positively impact their own work and the company's success.

4. Building a Culture of Resilience

Finally, one of the most important steps in managing uncertainty and resistance to change is building a culture of resilience. A resilient culture is one that embraces change, learns from challenges, and adapts quickly to new circumstances. In a PE-backed company, where the pace of change is often rapid, fostering resilience is critical to long-term success.

To build a resilient culture:

- **Encourage a Growth Mindset:** Employees should be encouraged to view change as an opportunity for growth, both personally and professionally. A growth mindset helps employees stay adaptable and open to new challenges.

- **Celebrate Small Wins:** Recognizing and celebrating small successes during the transition can help build momentum and keep employees motivated. Whether it's hitting a key performance target or successfully implementing a new process, small wins reinforce the idea that change can lead to positive outcomes.

- **Foster a Supportive Environment:** Employees are more

likely to embrace change when they feel supported by their colleagues and leadership. Fostering a collaborative, team-oriented environment can help employees navigate the transition together and build stronger bonds within the company.

Workshop Activities

Managing Resistance to Role Changes

Objective: Explore how to manage employee resistance to changes in roles and responsibilities during a post-acquisition transition.

Instructions:

- Think through a scenario where employees are resisting changes to their roles, such as increased reporting, new metrics to track, or additional oversight from the PE firm.

- Develop strategies for managing resistance, focusing on:

  » Communicating the benefits of the changes to the employees and the organization.

  » Providing support and resources for employees who are struggling to adapt.

  » Offering clear explanations of how the changes will impact their day-to-day work and how they can succeed in their new roles.

- Think about how to balance the need for change with maintaining employee morale and engagement.

Output: A resistance management plan that outlines how to address employee concerns and support them through role changes.

Actionable Takeaway: You will learn how to effectively manage employee resistance and ensure that role changes are implemented smoothly while keeping morale high.

Conclusion

Re-defining roles and responsibilities post-acquisition is one of the most significant challenges that companies face during a private equity transition. From adjusting to new reporting structures and managing relationships with PE owners to dealing with uncertainty and resistance to change, these shifts require thoughtful planning, clear communication, and strong leadership. By embracing new reporting systems, fostering strong relationships with the PE firm, and supporting employees through periods of uncertainty, companies can successfully navigate these changes and position themselves for long-term success. The key is to remain flexible, proactive, and focused on the shared goal of building a stronger, more competitive business.

DRIVING GROWTH AND CREATING VALUE

After the initial transition phase, the focus of any private equity (PE) acquisition shifts toward one critical goal: creating value. Private equity firms invest in companies with the expectation of driving significant growth and increasing profitability, and they do so through a combination of strategic initiatives, operational improvements, and financial engineering. For the management team and employees, this means that the pressure to perform and deliver results will increase as the company moves beyond the post-acquisition adjustment period and into the execution phase.

In this section, we will explore the strategies, tools, and frameworks that private equity firms use to drive growth and create value. From understanding the key performance metrics that PE firms track to setting and achieving ambitious growth targets, we'll delve into the specifics of how to align the company's operations with the goals of its new owners. Additionally, we'll examine how to strike the delicate balance between achieving short-term wins that satisfy the PE firm's immediate expectations and laying the groundwork for long-term, sustainable success.

CHAPTER 7

Performance Metrics and Accountability

"

When you measure what matters, accountability becomes the engine that drives growth and sustainable success.

"

At the heart of private equity's approach to driving growth and creating value is a deep focus on performance metrics and accountability. Private equity firms are relentless in their pursuit of measurable, data-driven results, and they expect the companies they acquire to adopt the same mindset. In this chapter, we will explore the key performance metrics that PE firms care about, how to set and achieve aggressive growth targets, and how to balance short-term wins with the company's long-term strategic vision.

The PE Playbook:
Key Metrics PE Firms Care About

Private equity firms rely heavily on performance metrics to track the progress of their portfolio companies and to make informed decisions about where to focus their efforts. These metrics serve as the foundation for the PE firm's investment thesis, and they are used to monitor the company's health, identify opportunities for improvement, and measure the success of value-creation initiatives.

Here are some of the key metrics that PE firms typically care about:

1. Revenue Growth

Revenue growth is one of the most important metrics for PE firms, as it is a direct indicator of the company's ability to expand and capture market share. PE firms often invest in companies with significant growth potential, and they expect to see top-line revenue increases year over year. This growth can come from various sources, including expanding into new markets, increasing sales to existing customers, launching new products, or pursuing strategic acquisitions.

For PE-backed companies, achieving consistent revenue growth is crucial to driving higher valuations and preparing the company for a successful exit. The PE firm will closely monitor monthly, quarterly, and annual revenue trends to ensure that the company is on track to meet its growth targets.

2. EBITDA and Profit Margins

Earnings before interest, taxes, depreciation, and

amortization (EBITDA) is a key metric that private equity firms use to assess a company's profitability. EBITDA provides a clear picture of the company's operating performance by excluding non-operational expenses like taxes and interest, allowing the PE firm to focus on the core earnings of the business.

In addition to EBITDA, PE firms are keenly interested in profit margins, including gross margins and operating margins. These metrics help the PE firm understand how efficiently the company is converting revenue into profit and identify opportunities to improve cost structures and increase profitability.

Improving EBITDA and profit margins is often one of the first areas of focus for PE firms after an acquisition. They may introduce operational improvements, renegotiate supplier contracts, or streamline production processes to drive higher margins and improve the company's overall financial performance.

3. Cash Flow and Working Capital

Cash flow is the lifeblood of any business, and PE firms pay close attention to a company's ability to generate consistent, positive cash flow. Positive cash flow ensures that the company can meet its financial obligations, invest in growth initiatives, and service any debt that may have been used to finance the acquisition.

In addition to overall cash flow, PE firms closely monitor working capital management. Efficient working capital management means that the company is effectively managing its short-term assets and liabilities, ensuring that it has enough liquidity to operate smoothly without tying up too much cash in inventory or accounts receivable.

4. Customer Acquisition Cost (CAC) and Lifetime Value (LTV)

For companies that rely on acquiring new customers to

drive growth, PE firms will closely track metrics related to customer acquisition and retention. Two of the most important metrics in this area are customer acquisition cost (CAC) and lifetime value (LTV).

- **CAC** measures how much the company is spending to acquire each new customer, including marketing and sales expenses. PE firms want to ensure that the company's customer acquisition efforts are cost-effective and that it is not overspending to win new business.

- **LTV** represents the total revenue that a customer is expected to generate over the course of their relationship with the company. A high LTV relative to CAC indicates that the company is acquiring valuable customers who will contribute to long-term profitability.

By optimizing these metrics, PE firms can help companies achieve more sustainable growth by focusing on acquiring high-value customers at a reasonable cost.

5. Debt Ratios and Leverage

In many private equity acquisitions, the company will take on significant debt to finance the buyout. As a result, PE firms pay close attention to debt ratios, such as the debt-to-equity ratio and the debt-to-EBITDA ratio, to ensure that the company is not over-leveraged and can comfortably service its debt obligations. A high level of leverage can increase the risk of financial distress, particularly if the company's cash flow or earnings decline unexpectedly. Private equity firms often use debt as a tool to enhance returns (known as financial leverage), but they also closely monitor the company's ability to meet interest payments and repay the principal. Managing debt levels is critical to ensuring the long-term financial health of the business.

6. Return on Investment (ROI) and Return on Equity (ROE)

At the end of the day, private equity firms are focused on generating strong returns for their investors. Key metrics like return on investment (ROI) and return on equity (ROE) are used to measure the effectiveness of the PE firm's investment strategy and the overall success of the acquisition.

- **ROI** measures the profitability of the PE firm's investment relative to the amount of capital invested.

- **ROE** assesses the return generated on the company's equity capital.

These metrics provide a clear picture of how well the company is performing and whether the investment is on track to meet the PE firm's financial goals.

Setting and Achieving

Aggressive Growth Targets

One of the defining characteristics of private equity ownership is the emphasis on setting and achieving aggressive growth targets. Private equity firms typically operate on a relatively short timeline, aiming to increase the company's value significantly within a three- to seven-year period before exiting the investment through a sale, IPO, or another transaction. As a result, PE firms push portfolio companies to achieve ambitious growth goals quickly.

Achieving these aggressive targets requires a combination of strategic planning, focused execution, and continuous performance monitoring. Let's break down how to set and achieve these targets in a PE-backed environment:

1. Setting Realistic but Ambitious Goals

PE firms work closely with the management team to establish aggressive growth targets that are achievable yet challenging. These goals are typically tied to increasing revenue, expanding market share, improving profitability, and driving operational efficiency.

When setting these goals, the company must strike a balance between ambition and realism. While private equity firms expect rapid growth, they also understand the importance of setting targets that are grounded in data and achievable given the company's market position, resources, and competitive landscape.

Examples of growth targets might include:

- Increasing top-line revenue by 20-30% per year

- Expanding into new geographic markets or customer segments

- Launching new products or services to drive incremental revenue

- Reducing production costs by 10-15% through process improvements

To ensure that these targets are realistic, the company's management team must conduct a thorough analysis of the market, assess internal capabilities, and consider potential risks and barriers to success.

2. Breaking Down Targets into Actionable Steps

Once growth targets have been established, the next step is to break them down into actionable steps that can be executed at every level of the organization. This involves creating a detailed growth plan that outlines the specific initiatives, investments, and resources required to achieve each target.

For example, if the company's goal is to increase revenue by 25%, this might involve:

- Expanding the sales team and setting aggressive sales quotas

- Investing in marketing campaigns to drive lead generation and brand awareness

- Improving customer retention by enhancing the customer experience or offering new services

- Exploring potential partnerships or acquisitions to enter new markets

By breaking down high-level targets into specific, actionable steps, the management team can ensure that everyone in the organization is aligned and working toward the same goals.

3. Assigning Accountability for Key Results

In a PE-backed company, accountability is paramount. Every member of the management team and every department within the organization must have clearly defined responsibilities and metrics for success. This ensures that everyone is held accountable for achieving their portion of the overall growth target.

For example:

- The sales team may be responsible for delivering a certain percentage of revenue growth by hitting sales quotas.

- The marketing team might be tasked with driving a specific number of leads or achieving a certain conversion rate.

- The operations team might be responsible for reducing production costs by improving efficiency or negotiating better supplier terms.

By assigning accountability at every level, the company can ensure that progress is being made across all departments and that no one is left out of the process.

4. Measuring Progress and Adjusting Course

Regularly measuring progress is critical to ensuring that the company stays on track to achieve its aggressive growth targets. Private equity firms expect frequent updates on performance, and the management team must establish a robust system for tracking key performance metrics and making adjustments as needed.

Monthly or quarterly reviews provide an opportunity to assess whether the company is meeting its targets, identify any areas where performance is lagging, and make necessary adjustments to the strategy. For example, if revenue growth is falling short of expectations, the company might need to ramp up marketing efforts, invest in additional sales resources, or explore new market opportunities.

Continuous improvement is key in this process. The company must be willing to adapt quickly and pivot when necessary to stay on track for achieving its growth targets.

How to Balance Short-Term Wins with Long-Term Strategy

In a private equity environment, there is often a strong focus on achieving short-term wins that demonstrate immediate progress and deliver quick returns. However, it's equally important to balance these short-term gains with a long-term strategy that ensures sustainable growth and lasting value creation.

Here's how to strike the right balance:

1. Focusing on Quick Wins That Build Momentum

Private equity firms often prioritize quick wins–initiatives that can be implemented rapidly and generate immediate results. These quick wins might include cutting unnecessary costs, renegotiating supplier contracts, or streamlining operations to improve profitability.

Quick wins are important because they build momentum, create buy-in from employees and stakeholders, and demonstrate to the PE firm that the company is capable of delivering results. However, it's crucial that these quick wins do not come at the expense of long-term success.

Examples of quick wins include:

- Reducing overhead costs by cutting discretionary spending or eliminating non-essential roles

- Improving cash flow by optimizing working capital management or accelerating customer payments

- Increasing sales through targeted promotional campaigns or upselling existing customers

2. Avoiding Short-Term Fixes That Undermine Long-Term Growth

While short-term wins are valuable, it's important to avoid the temptation to focus solely on short-term fixes that could undermine the company's long-term growth potential. For example, cutting R&D spending or delaying investments in new technologies might boost short-term profitability but could hinder the company's ability to innovate and remain competitive in the future.

To avoid this pitfall, the management team must evaluate each decision through the lens of both short-term and long-term impact. Initiatives that generate immediate returns should be pursued, but not at the expense of the company's ability to invest in future growth opportunities.

3. Investing in Long-Term Value Drivers

While private equity firms expect short-term wins, they are also focused on building a company that can sustain growth over the long term. This means investing in value drivers that will contribute to the company's future success, such as innovation, talent development, and market expansion.

Examples of long-term value drivers include:

- **Innovation:** Investing in R&D to develop new products or services that will differentiate the company in the market and drive future revenue growth.

- **Talent Development:** Building a strong leadership team and investing in employee training and development to ensure that the company has the skills and capabilities needed to execute on its long-term strategy.

- **Market Expansion:** Exploring opportunities to enter new geographic markets or customer segments that offer significant growth potential.

By investing in these long-term value drivers, the company can build a strong foundation for sustainable growth while still delivering on the short-term goals set by the PE firm.

4. Maintaining a Long-Term Vision

Finally, it's essential for the company's leadership team to maintain a long-term vision for the business, even as they focus on delivering short-term results. This long-term vision should serve as a guiding framework for all decision-making, ensuring that the company stays true to its core values and strategic objectives.

Regular communication with the PE firm about the company's long-term goals can help ensure alignment and prevent an overemphasis on short-term gains. While the pressure to deliver immediate results will always be present, a strong long-term vision ensures that the company remains focused on creating lasting value for all stakeholders.

Workshop Activities

Managing Underperformance and Adjusting Targets

Objective: Develop a plan for managing underperformance and adjusting growth targets when key metrics are not met.

Instructions:

- Think through a scenario in which a company is underperforming on key metrics (e.g., EBITDA is lower than projected, revenue growth is stagnant).

- Task yourself with:

  » Identifying the reasons for underperformance (e.g., operational inefficiencies, market challenges, leadership issues).

  » Developing a plan to address these challenges and improve performance in the next quarter.

  » Adjusting growth targets if necessary and creating a revised strategy to achieve long-term goals.

- Write out your recovery plan, explaining how you will manage underperformance and get the company back on track.

Output: A recovery plan that addresses underperformance, adjusts targets, and outlines specific steps to improve performance in the next quarter.

Actionable Takeaway: You will gain experience in managing underperformance and adjusting targets while staying aligned with long-term goals.

Conclusion

Performance metrics and accountability are the foundation of private equity's approach to driving growth and creating value. By focusing on key metrics like revenue growth, EBITDA, cash flow, and customer acquisition costs, private equity firms are able to measure progress and ensure that their portfolio companies are on track to achieve aggressive growth targets.

Balancing the need for short-term wins with a focus on long-term strategy is critical to building a company that can sustain growth beyond the PE firm's investment horizon. By investing in both quick wins and long-term value drivers, the management team can ensure that the company is well-positioned for success in both the short and long term.

CHAPTER 8

Operational Improvements and Cost Efficiency

"

Streamlining operations isn't just about cutting costs—it's about building a foundation for innovation, efficiency, and growth.

"

In private equity, operational efficiency is essential for value creation. Upon acquiring a company, private equity firms prioritize making the business leaner and more profitable through cost efficiency to support long-term growth. This involves optimizing processes, leveraging technology, and identifying overlooked cost-saving opportunities. This chapter outlines how private equity firms approach operational improvements and cost efficiency. It discusses strategies for streamlining processes, the role of technology in enhancing efficiency, and techniques for uncovering and exploiting cost-saving opportunities without sacrificing quality or growth potential.

Process Optimization: Making Leaner, Faster Operations

At the core of any operational improvement initiative is process optimization. Private equity firms focus on identifying inefficiencies in the company's operations, refining existing processes, and implementing new workflows that allow the business to operate more efficiently. The goal is to reduce waste, improve productivity, and create a leaner, faster organization that can better compete in the market.

1. Conducting a Comprehensive Process Audit

The first step in process optimization is to conduct a comprehensive audit of the company's existing operations. This audit provides a clear understanding of how the business is currently functioning, identifies areas of inefficiency, and highlights opportunities for improvement. The process audit typically covers every aspect of the company's operations, including:

- **Production and Manufacturing:** Are production lines running at full capacity? Are there any bottlenecks slowing down the manufacturing process?

- **Supply Chain Management:** Is the supply chain efficient and cost-effective? Are there delays in the procurement process or issues with inventory management?

- **Sales and Marketing:** How effective are the current sales processes in converting leads into customers? Is the marketing team generating qualified leads at a reasonable cost?

- **Customer Service:** Are customer service processes streamlined, or are there unnecessary steps that slow down response times?

Once the audit is complete, the company's leadership team can begin to prioritize areas for improvement based on their impact on the company's bottom line and overall efficiency.

2. Lean Methodology and Process Reengineering

Private equity firms often introduce lean methodologies and process reengineering as a way to optimize operations. Lean thinking focuses on reducing waste and maximizing value by streamlining processes and eliminating non-value-added activities. This approach can be applied to any part of the organization, from production lines to back-office functions.

Some common lean strategies include:

- **Value Stream Mapping:** Value stream mapping is a tool used to visualize the flow of materials and information through the company's operations. By mapping out each step of the process, the company can identify areas where time, resources, or effort are being wasted.

- **Continuous Improvement (Kaizen):** Continuous improvement is a core principle of lean methodology. It encourages employees at all levels to identify and implement small, incremental changes that improve efficiency and reduce waste. Over time, these small improvements add up to significant gains in productivity and cost savings.

- **Eliminating Bottlenecks:** Process bottlenecks are points in the workflow where progress is slowed or halted due to inefficiencies or constraints. These bottlenecks can lead to delays, increased costs, and reduced productivity. By identifying and addressing these bottlenecks, the company can increase throughput and improve overall performance.

- **Standardization:** Standardizing processes helps ensure that tasks are completed consistently and efficiently. By creating standard operating procedures (SOPs) for key functions, companies can reduce variability, improve quality, and increase efficiency.

3. Implementing Automation

Automation plays a significant role in process optimization by allowing companies to complete tasks more quickly, accurately, and with fewer resources. Automation can be applied to a wide range of functions, from production lines and logistics to administrative tasks and customer interactions.

Examples of automation include:

- **Robotic Process Automation (RPA):** RPA uses software robots to automate repetitive tasks, such as data entry, invoice processing, or customer service interactions. By automating these routine tasks, companies can free up employees to focus on more value-added activities and reduce the risk of human error.

- **Automated Manufacturing Systems:** In manufacturing environments, automation can take the form of robotics, automated conveyor systems, and advanced machinery that increase production speed and precision. Automated systems can also help reduce labor costs and improve overall production efficiency.

- **Automated Customer Interactions:** Automation can also be applied to customer-facing functions, such as chatbots or automated email responses. These tools can handle routine inquiries, allowing customer service representatives to focus on more complex issues.

Automation not only improves efficiency but also enhances scalability. As the company grows, automated systems can handle increased workloads without the need for additional staff or resources.

Technology as a Driver for Efficiency

In today's fast-paced business environment, technology is a critical driver of efficiency and operational improvements. Private equity firms often invest in technology upgrades or implement new technologies to help portfolio companies streamline their operations, improve decision-making, and reduce costs. The right technology infrastructure can enable a company to scale more quickly, improve accuracy, and respond to market changes with agility.

1. Enterprise Resource Planning (ERP) Systems

One of the most common technology investments made by private equity firms is the implementation of an Enterprise Resource Planning (ERP) system. An ERP system integrates various business processes—such as finance, HR, procurement, inventory management, and supply chain operations—into a single, unified platform. This integration allows for better visibility, coordination, and decision-making across the organization.

Benefits of an ERP system include:

- **Improved Data Accuracy and Accessibility:** An ERP system centralizes data from different departments, providing a single source of truth. This improves data accuracy and ensures that decision-makers have access to real-time information.

- **Enhanced Efficiency:** By automating routine tasks, such as order processing, invoicing, and inventory management, an ERP system reduces manual work and streamlines operations.

- **Better Decision-Making:** With real-time access to data, managers can make more informed decisions about everything from resource allocation to production scheduling. ERP systems also provide valuable insights into key performance metrics, allowing the company to identify trends and address potential issues more quickly.

- **Scalability:** As the company grows, an ERP system can easily scale to accommodate new locations, products, or services, ensuring that the business continues to operate efficiently.

2. Cloud-Based Solutions

Cloud technology has revolutionized the way businesses operate, providing increased flexibility, scalability, and cost-efficiency. By leveraging cloud-based solutions, private equity firms can help companies improve their IT infrastructure without the need for significant upfront capital investment.

Key advantages of cloud-based solutions include:

- **Scalability:** Cloud-based platforms can scale up or down based on the company's needs, making them ideal for businesses that experience fluctuating demand or rapid growth.

- **Cost Savings:** Cloud solutions often operate on a subscription-based model, allowing companies to pay for only the resources they use. This eliminates the need for large, upfront investments in hardware or software.

- **Remote Accessibility:** Cloud-based systems enable employees to access information and collaborate from anywhere, making them particularly valuable for companies with distributed workforces or remote teams.

- **Improved Collaboration:** Cloud platforms make it easier for teams to collaborate in real-time, share documents, and manage projects, regardless of their location.

3. Data Analytics and Business Intelligence Tools

In the private equity world, data-driven decision-making is key to success. To optimize operations and improve efficiency, companies need access to accurate, actionable insights that can inform their strategy and guide their decision-making. Business intelligence (BI) tools and data analytics platforms provide this visibility, allowing companies to analyze large volumes of data, identify trends, and make more informed decisions.

Benefits of data analytics and BI tools include:

- **Real-Time Performance Monitoring:** BI tools allow companies to track key performance indicators (KPIs) in real-time, providing immediate visibility into how the business is performing. This enables managers to respond quickly to issues, adjust strategies, and optimize operations on the fly.

- **Predictive Analytics:** Advanced analytics tools can help companies forecast future demand, identify potential risks, and anticipate market trends. By leveraging predictive analytics, companies can make proactive decisions that drive long-term growth.

- **Improved Resource Allocation:** Data analytics tools provide insights into resource utilization, enabling companies to allocate labor, capital, and other resources more efficiently. This helps reduce waste and ensures that the company is operating at peak efficiency.

- **Enhanced Customer Insights:** For customer-facing businesses, data analytics platforms can provide valuable insights into customer behavior, preferences, and purchasing patterns. This information can be used to optimize marketing strategies, improve product offerings, and increase customer satisfaction.

Identifying and Capitalizing on Cost-Saving Opportunities

Private equity firms are known for their ability to identify and capitalize on cost-saving opportunities. Whether through process improvements, renegotiating contracts, or optimizing the supply chain, PE firms focus on reducing costs without compromising the quality of products or services. The goal is to increase profitability by streamlining operations and eliminating unnecessary expenses.

1. Reviewing and Renegotiating Supplier Contracts

One of the first areas where private equity firms look for cost-saving opportunities is supplier contracts. Many companies maintain long-standing relationships with suppliers, but these contracts may not always be optimized for cost-efficiency. A thorough review of supplier agreements can reveal opportunities to renegotiate pricing, improve payment terms, or switch to alternative suppliers that offer better value.

Steps for optimizing supplier contracts:

- **Conduct a Market Comparison:** Compare the pricing and terms offered by current suppliers with those available in the broader market. This provides leverage for negotiating better deals.

- **Consolidate Suppliers:** In some cases, consolidating multiple suppliers into a single contract can provide economies of scale, reducing overall costs and simplifying the procurement process.

- **Negotiate Payment Terms:** Improving payment terms, such as securing early payment discounts or extending payment deadlines, can improve cash flow and reduce costs.

2. Optimizing Inventory Management

Inventory management is another area where significant cost savings can be achieved. Inefficient inventory management can lead to overstocking, increased carrying costs, and wasted resources. By optimizing inventory levels and implementing just-in-time (JIT) inventory practices, companies can reduce excess inventory and free up working capital.

Strategies for optimizing inventory management include:

- **Implementing Inventory Tracking Systems:** Modern inventory tracking systems provide real-time visibility into stock levels, helping companies avoid overstocking and reduce carrying costs.

- **Just-in-Time (JIT) Inventory:** JIT inventory systems ensure that materials are delivered only when they are needed for production, minimizing storage costs and reducing the risk of obsolescence.

- **Demand Forecasting:** Accurate demand forecasting allows companies to adjust inventory levels based on expected demand, reducing the need for emergency orders or rush shipments.

3. Reducing Overhead Costs

Overhead costs, such as rent, utilities, and administrative expenses, can significantly impact a company's profitability. Private equity firms often look for ways to reduce these fixed costs, either by renegotiating contracts, outsourcing non-core functions, or consolidating operations.

Examples of overhead cost-saving initiatives include:

- **Real Estate Optimization:** By consolidating office or production facilities, companies can reduce rent and utility expenses. In some cases, moving to a more cost-effective location may also provide additional savings.

- **Outsourcing Non-Core Functions:** Outsourcing functions such as IT support, payroll processing, or HR services can reduce administrative costs and allow the company to focus on its core business activities.

- **Implementing Energy-Efficiency Measures:** Investing in energy-efficient equipment, upgrading lighting systems, or renegotiating utility contracts can lead to significant cost savings over time.

4. Improving Labor Efficiency

Labor costs are often one of the largest expenses for any company. Improving labor efficiency, either by optimizing workforce scheduling or investing in employee training and development, can help reduce costs while maintaining productivity.

Ways to improve labor efficiency:

- **Optimizing Scheduling:** Ensuring that employees are scheduled based on peak demand times can reduce unnecessary labor costs and improve productivity.

- **Cross-Training Employees:** Cross-training employees to perform multiple functions can reduce the need for additional staff and increase operational flexibility.

- **Investing in Training and Development:** Well-trained employees are more productive and less likely to make costly mistakes. Investing in employee training can lead to long-term cost savings by improving overall performance and reducing turnover.

Workshop Activities

Cost-Saving Opportunity Identification

Objective: Learn how to identify and implement cost-saving opportunities across different areas of the business.

Instructions:

- Come up with a fictional company financial profile that includes cost breakdowns for various departments (e.g., manufacturing, marketing, logistics, HR).

- Identify cost-saving opportunities in specific areas of the business, such as:
  » Reducing overhead costs.
  » Negotiating better terms with suppliers.
  » Outsourcing non-core activities.
  » Implementing energy-saving initiatives.
- Develop a cost-saving plan, outlining specific actions the company can take to reduce costs without compromising quality or customer satisfaction.

Output: A cost-saving plan that identifies key opportunities for reducing costs and outlines actionable steps to implement these changes.

Actionable Takeaway: You will learn how to assess company financials, identify cost-saving opportunities, and create actionable plans for reducing costs while maintaining operational effectiveness.

Conclusion

Operational improvements and cost efficiency are critical components of value creation in a private equity-backed company. By optimizing processes, leveraging technology, and identifying cost-saving opportunities, companies can improve productivity, reduce waste, and increase profitability. Private equity firms bring a disciplined, data-driven approach to operational improvements, focusing on measurable results and sustainable efficiency gains. For companies navigating the post-acquisition transition, embracing these improvements is essential to achieving long-term success and maximizing value for all stakeholders.

CHAPTER 9

Talent Management and Retention Strategies

> *The key to success post-acquisition lies in retaining and empowering your top talent to drive the company's vision forward.*

Post-acquisition, one of the most critical aspects of driving long-term success is managing talent effectively. Private equity (PE) firms know that behind every business are the people who execute the strategy, drive innovation, and maintain the operational engine. Without the right talent, even the most well-crafted financial plans and operational improvements can fall short.

Talent management and retention become especially important in the high-pressure environment of a private equity-backed company, where rapid growth and performance improvements are expected. This chapter focuses on how to incentivize key personnel post-acquisition, retain and attract top talent in a demanding environment, and align employee goals with the private equity firm's expectations.

Incentivizing Key Personnel

Post-Acquisition

When a private equity firm acquires a company, one of the first areas they often focus on is ensuring that key personnel stay motivated and aligned with the new strategic goals. These individuals are usually critical to the company's continued success, as they possess deep institutional knowledge and play pivotal roles in operations, sales, marketing, finance, or product development. Losing them can disrupt the business and undermine the firm's ability to execute its post-acquisition strategy.

1. Understanding the Importance of Key Personnel

Key personnel often include the executive team, senior managers, and other employees who are instrumental in keeping the business running smoothly and driving growth. These individuals are often deeply invested in the company's operations, customer relationships, and culture. If they leave post-acquisition, the company could experience disruptions that make it difficult to achieve the aggressive growth targets set by the PE firm.

Private equity firms recognize that without retaining these key employees, they face a significant risk of operational inefficiency and a longer path to return on investment (ROI). As a result, talent management efforts post-acquisition start with identifying these essential team members and taking proactive steps to incentivize them.

2. Developing Financial Incentive Plans

One of the most common strategies PE firms use to retain key personnel is by implementing financial incentive plans. These plans align the interests of the employees with the performance goals of the company and ensure that the most important people are rewarded for helping the company achieve its financial and operational objectives.

Common financial incentive structures include:

- **Equity Compensation:** Offering equity or stock options is a powerful tool in aligning employee interests with those of the private equity firm. By giving key employees a direct stake in the company's future success, they are incentivized to work toward increasing the company's value. Equity compensation also encourages longer tenures, as employees often need to stay for a certain period to fully vest their shares.

- **Performance-Based Bonuses:** Tying bonuses to specific performance metrics is another effective way to incentivize employees post-acquisition. These metrics could be tied to revenue growth, profitability (EBITDA), operational efficiency, or individual KPIs. By providing bonuses based on achieving certain milestones, key personnel remain focused on meeting the PE firm's objectives.

- **Retention Bonuses:** In addition to performance-based bonuses, some PE firms offer retention bonuses as a way to keep key employees on board through the transition and the early stages of post-acquisition integration. These bonuses are typically paid out over a set period, ensuring that critical talent remains with the company during the most important phases of the transformation.

3. Offering Non-Financial Incentives

While financial incentives are important, they are not the only tool PE firms and management teams have at their disposal to retain key talent. Non-financial incentives can also play a significant role in keeping employees motivated, engaged, and committed to the company's success.

Examples of non-financial incentives include:

- **Career Development Opportunities:** Many key employees are motivated by career advancement and personal growth. Offering development opportunities, such as leadership training, mentorship programs, or access to executive coaching, can be a powerful way to retain top talent. These opportunities demonstrate that the company is invested in the long-term success of its people, even during periods of change.

- **Work-Life Balance and Flexibility:** Post-acquisition, the pressure to perform often increases, and burnout can become a real risk. Offering flexible work arrangements, such as remote work options or adjusted hours, can help mitigate stress and show employees that their well-being is a priority. This is particularly important in today's work environment, where flexible arrangements are increasingly valued by top talent.

- **Recognition and Purpose:** High-performing employees want to feel valued and recognized for their contributions. Acknowledging their efforts through public recognition, awards, or personal feedback from leadership can boost morale and create a stronger connection to the company's mission and objectives. Additionally, providing a sense of purpose by clearly communicating how their work contributes to the company's long-term goals helps employees stay engaged.

How to Retain and Attract Top Talent in a High-Pressure Environment

Private equity acquisitions often come with a heightened sense of urgency, as the new owners work to implement growth strategies, streamline operations, and improve financial performance. This environment can put significant pressure on employees, particularly those in leadership and key management positions. Retaining and attracting top talent in such an environment requires thoughtful strategies that go beyond simply offering competitive compensation.

1. Building a Culture of High Performance and Accountability

Private equity firms thrive on performance, and companies under PE ownership must quickly adapt to a results-driven culture. This can be a major shift for employees who are used to a slower pace or more informal goal-setting processes. To retain and attract top talent in this environment, it's essential to foster a culture of high performance and accountability.

Key elements of a high-performance culture include:

- **Clear Performance Metrics:** Employees need to understand exactly what is expected of them and how their performance will be measured. This clarity helps eliminate ambiguity and allows top talent to focus on achieving specific goals. By providing clear KPIs and regular performance reviews, companies can ensure that their teams are aligned with strategic objectives.

- **Empowerment and Ownership:** Top talent thrives in environments where they feel empowered to make decisions and take ownership of their work. Private equity firms should encourage a culture of autonomy, where employees are trusted to execute on their responsibilities without micromanagement. This sense of ownership can be particularly motivating for high achievers who want to make a tangible impact on the company's success.

- **Accountability Systems:** While autonomy is important, so is accountability. Employees at all levels should be held accountable for their performance, and there should be clear consequences for missing targets or underperforming. This ensures that the entire organization is aligned with the PE firm's growth objectives and that top talent remains engaged and motivated to deliver results.

2. Creating a Compelling Employer Brand

Attracting top talent in a high-pressure environment requires more than just offering competitive salaries and bonuses. Companies must also create a compelling employer brand that differentiates them from competitors and attracts high-caliber candidates who are eager to work in a fast-paced, results-oriented culture.

Building a strong employer brand involves:

- **Highlighting Career Growth Opportunities:** Private equity-backed companies often experience rapid growth, which can provide significant opportunities for career advancement. Companies should position themselves as a place where ambitious professionals can accelerate their careers and take on leadership roles.

- **Emphasizing Impact and Purpose:** Top talent wants to know that their work matters. By communicating the company's mission, values, and long-term vision, companies can attract employees who are motivated by more than just financial rewards. Demonstrating how the company is making a positive impact on its industry, community, or customers can be a powerful way to attract talent that is aligned with the company's goals.

- **Showcasing Success Stories:** Sharing success stories of employees who have thrived in the private equity-backed environment can help reinforce the company's employer brand. These stories can illustrate how individuals have grown their careers, taken on new challenges, and contributed to the company's overall success. They can also provide a roadmap for potential hires, showing them what is possible within the organization.

3. Addressing Employee Stress and Burnout

High-pressure environments can lead to employee burnout if not managed carefully. Long hours, aggressive performance targets, and constant change can take a toll on employees' well-being. Retaining top talent requires a proactive approach to managing stress and preventing burnout.

Strategies to manage employee stress include:

- **Offering Mental Health and Wellness Programs:** Providing access to mental health resources, such as counseling services or wellness programs, can help employees cope with the demands of the job.

Encouraging regular breaks, promoting work-life balance, and fostering a supportive workplace culture can also alleviate stress.

- **Creating a Supportive Leadership Team:** Employees look to their leaders for guidance and support, especially in high-pressure environments. Managers should be trained to recognize signs of burnout and take steps to address it before it becomes a bigger issue. Regular check-ins with team members, open communication, and a focus on employee well-being can go a long way in maintaining morale and productivity.

- **Flexible Work Arrangements:** Offering flexible work arrangements, such as remote work or adjusted hours, can help employees manage their workload more effectively. In a high-pressure environment, giving employees control over how and when they work can reduce stress and increase job satisfaction.

Aligning Employee Goals with PE Expectations

One of the most critical aspects of talent management in a private equity-backed company is ensuring that employee goals are aligned with the expectations of the PE firm. Private equity firms have a clear vision for the company's future, and it's essential that every employee understands how their role contributes to the achievement of these objectives. When employee goals are aligned with the company's strategic plan, the entire organization can work together more effectively to drive growth and create value.

1. Communicating the Company's Strategic Vision

Private equity firms often bring a new strategic vision to the companies they acquire. This vision typically includes aggressive growth targets, operational improvements, and a focus on increasing profitability. To align employee goals with these expectations, the company's leadership team must clearly communicate the new strategic direction and explain how it impacts each department and individual.

Steps for communicating the strategic vision:

- **Town Hall Meetings:** Holding company-wide town hall meetings where leadership outlines the strategic vision can help employees understand the big picture. These meetings provide an opportunity for employees to ask questions, voice concerns, and gain clarity on how the company's goals will be achieved.

- **Departmental Breakdowns:** After the overarching vision is communicated, department heads should break it down into specific goals and targets for their teams. This ensures that each department understands its role in contributing to the company's success.

- **Ongoing Communication:** The strategic vision should not be a one-time announcement. Regular updates from leadership, along with progress reports on key initiatives, help keep employees engaged and aligned with the company's evolving objectives.

2. Setting Individual and Team Goals

Once the company's strategic vision has been communicated, the next step is to align individual and team goals with the private equity firm's expectations. Employees need to understand how their daily work contributes to the larger objectives and what specific goals they are expected to achieve.

Steps for setting aligned goals:

- **SMART Goals:** Individual and team goals should be SMART—Specific, Measurable, Achievable, Relevant, and Time-bound. This ensures that employees have clear, actionable targets that align with the company's overall strategy.

- **Linking Goals to KPIs:** Each employee's goals should be directly tied to the key performance indicators (KPIs) that the private equity firm is tracking. Whether it's increasing sales, improving operational efficiency, or reducing costs, employees should know exactly how their work impacts the company's performance metrics.

- **Regular Performance Reviews:** Performance reviews provide an opportunity to assess whether employees are on track to meet their goals and make adjustments as needed. These reviews should be data-driven and focused on measurable outcomes that align with the company's strategic objectives.

3. Providing Ongoing Feedback and Recognition

Employees are more likely to stay engaged and motivated when they receive regular feedback on their performance and are recognized for their contributions. In a high-pressure environment, it's easy for feedback to become focused solely on areas for improvement, but positive reinforcement is just as important for maintaining morale.

Best practices for providing feedback and recognition:

- **Regular Check-Ins:** Managers should schedule regular one-on-one check-ins with their team members to provide feedback on their progress toward goals. These check-ins offer an opportunity to celebrate successes, address challenges, and adjust goals if necessary.

- **Public Recognition:** Recognizing employees publicly for their achievements can boost morale and motivate others to perform at a high level. This could be done through team meetings, company-wide emails, or recognition programs that reward outstanding performance.

- **Constructive Feedback:** When providing constructive feedback, it's important to focus on solutions rather than simply pointing out problems. Employees should leave feedback sessions with a clear understanding of what they can do to improve and how their efforts will contribute to the company's success.

Workshop Activities

Creating a Culture of Performance and Accountability

Objective: Develop strategies to create a culture of performance and accountability aligned with private equity expectations.

Instructions:

- Develop a case study where the PE firm has set high expectations for performance, but the company's culture is not fully aligned with these expectations.

- Create a plan to shift the company culture toward one of high performance and accountability by:
  - » Setting clear performance expectations and goals for employees at every level.
  - » Creating performance metrics and KPIs that are tracked
  - » Implementing a feedback and review system to ensure employees are held accountable for meeting their goals.
  - » Providing rewards and recognition for high performers and addressing underperformance in a fair and supportive manner.
- Have a plan showing culture shift, explaining how you will create a high-performance culture while maintaining employee morale and engagement.

Output: A culture shift plan that aligns employee performance with the private equity firm's expectations while fostering accountability and motivation.

Actionable Takeaway: You will learn how to create a culture of performance and accountability that motivates employees to meet the company's strategic objectives.

Conclusion

Talent management and retention are critical components of driving success in a private equity-backed company. By incentivizing key personnel, retaining and attracting top talent in a high-pressure environment, and aligning employee goals with the private equity firm's expectations, companies can build a strong, motivated workforce that is ready to execute on the strategic vision. Post-acquisition, the stakes are high, and ensuring that the right people are in place—and motivated to perform—is essential to achieving the aggressive growth targets set by the private equity firm. Through a combination of financial incentives, non-financial rewards, clear communication, and ongoing support, companies can create an environment where top talent thrives and contributes to the company's long-term success.

SCALING FOR SUCCESS

Once a private equity acquisition has stabilized, the next critical focus is scaling the business to maximize growth and drive long-term value. For private equity firms, scaling is not just about growing incrementally—it's about accelerating growth in a way that significantly increases the company's value within a relatively short timeframe. This requires the management team to implement carefully crafted strategies that leverage the company's strengths while capitalizing on new opportunities.

Scaling a business involves more than just increasing revenues; it requires strategic decisions around market expansion, product diversification, operational efficiency, and potential acquisitions. The right scaling strategy aligns with both short-term and long-term goals, ensuring that the company grows sustainably without sacrificing profitability or operational excellence.

In this section, we will explore the key strategies and best practices for scaling a business under private equity ownership. Whether it's expanding product lines, entering new markets, or forming strategic partnerships, the chapters ahead will provide a roadmap for companies looking to grow successfully and create long-term value.

CHAPTER 10

Strategies for Scaling The Business

"

Scaling smartly requires a balance of ambition, strategy, and the right partnerships to transform growth potential into reality.

"

Scaling a business is a complex process that requires careful planning, execution, and continuous refinement. For companies backed by private equity, scaling is not just a growth imperative—it's a strategic necessity. The private equity firm's investment thesis is often built around the company's potential for rapid, scalable growth, and the management team must deliver on these expectations. However, scaling too quickly or without a solid plan can lead to operational inefficiencies, financial strain, and even failure.

In this chapter, we will cover the essential components of building and executing a scalable growth plan, how to expand product lines and enter new markets, and the role of strategic partnerships and acquisitions in accelerating growth.

Building and Executing
a Scalable Growth Plan

Scaling a business starts with a well-constructed growth plan that outlines the company's goals, the strategies to achieve them, and the resources required for execution. This plan serves as the blueprint for the company's expansion efforts and provides a clear roadmap for all stakeholders involved.

1. Identifying Growth Opportunities

Before executing any growth plan, it's essential to identify the most viable opportunities for scaling. This involves conducting a thorough analysis of the market, competitors, customer needs, and the company's internal capabilities.

Key areas to assess when identifying growth opportunities include:

- **Market Demand:** Is there a growing demand for the company's products or services in existing markets? Are there underserved or untapped markets that the company can enter? Understanding market trends and customer behavior is critical for identifying areas where growth is feasible.

- **Competitive Landscape:** How does the company stack up against its competitors? Are there gaps in the market where the company can differentiate itself? Analyzing the competitive landscape helps identify opportunities to gain market share.

- **Internal Capabilities:** Does the company have the necessary infrastructure, talent, and resources to support growth? Are there areas where additional investment or expertise is needed to scale effectively?

Once growth opportunities have been identified, the next step is to prioritize them based on potential impact and alignment with the company's strategic objectives.

2. Setting Scalable Growth Targets

Private equity firms expect aggressive growth, but it's important to set targets that are both ambitious and achievable. Setting unrealistic goals can lead to overextension, while conservative targets may not unlock the company's full potential.

Scalable growth targets should be:

- **Data-Driven:** Growth targets should be based on data, including historical performance, market trends, and customer demand. This ensures that the targets are grounded in reality and that the company is pursuing opportunities with the highest potential for success.

- **Aligned with Long-Term Strategy:** While scaling quickly is important, growth targets must align with the company's long-term vision and objectives. Short-term wins are valuable, but they should not come at the expense of long-term sustainability.

- **Measurable and Trackable:** Setting specific, measurable growth targets allows the company to monitor progress and make adjustments as needed. Key performance indicators (KPIs) should be established to track revenue growth, customer acquisition, profitability, and other critical metrics.

3. Ensuring Operational Scalability

A common mistake companies make when scaling is focusing solely on revenue growth without considering whether their operations can support that growth. Scaling requires more than just selling more products or entering new markets—it requires operational efficiency and the ability to handle increased demand without sacrificing quality or service.

Steps to ensure operational scalability include:

- **Investing in Infrastructure:** As the company grows, it may need to invest in new facilities, equipment, or technology to support higher production volumes, expanded distribution networks, or increased customer service capacity. Failing to make these investments can lead to bottlenecks and inefficiencies.

- **Standardizing Processes:** Standardizing processes across the organization is essential for maintaining quality and consistency as the company scales. This involves creating standard operating procedures (SOPs) for key functions, such as production, sales, and customer service, to ensure that the business can operate smoothly even as demand increases.

- **Leveraging Technology:** Technology plays a critical role in scaling operations. Implementing automation, upgrading ERP systems, and utilizing data analytics can help the company operate more efficiently and handle higher volumes of business without overburdening its resources.

4. Building a Scalable Team

Scaling the business also requires scaling the team. The company will need the right talent in place to execute its growth strategy, from leadership to frontline employees.

This may involve hiring new staff, restructuring existing teams, or investing in employee development programs to ensure that the workforce has the skills needed to support the company's expansion.

Key considerations for building a scalable team include:

- **Talent Acquisition:** As the company grows, it will need to attract top talent with the expertise and experience to drive growth. This may involve hiring senior leaders with a track record of scaling businesses or expanding the sales and marketing teams to support increased demand.

- **Training and Development:** Existing employees should be given opportunities to develop new skills and take on greater responsibilities as the company scales. Providing ongoing training and leadership development programs can help ensure that the company's talent pool evolves in step with its growth trajectory.

- **Cultural Alignment:** It's important to maintain a strong company culture even as the organization grows. A scalable growth plan should include strategies for preserving the company's core values and culture while integrating new employees and adapting to new challenges.

Expanding Product Lines and
Entering New Markets

Expanding product lines and entering new markets are two of the most effective ways to scale a business. These strategies not only increase revenue streams but also help diversify the company's portfolio and reduce dependence on any single market or product.

1. Expanding Product Lines

Expanding the company's product offerings can significantly accelerate growth by allowing the business to capture new customer segments, increase average order values, and enhance its competitive positioning. However, product expansion requires careful planning to ensure that the company is investing in products that align with customer demand and its long-term strategy.

Steps to successfully expand product lines include:

- **Market Research:** Conducting thorough market research is essential for identifying new product opportunities. The company must understand customer needs, preferences, and pain points to develop products that meet demand and provide a competitive edge.

- **Leveraging Existing Capabilities:** When expanding product lines, companies should consider products that leverage their existing capabilities, resources, and expertise. This reduces the risk and cost associated with product development and allows the company to bring new offerings to market more quickly.

- **Testing and Iterating:** Before launching a new product at scale, it's important to test it in the market. This could involve conducting a pilot program or launching the product in a limited region to gather feedback and refine the offering before a full rollout.

2. Entering New Markets

Expanding into new geographic markets is another powerful way to scale the business. Whether it's entering new regions within the country or expanding internationally, market expansion offers opportunities to grow the customer base and diversify revenue streams. However, market entry requires careful consideration of local market conditions, regulatory environments, and cultural differences.

Key steps for successful market entry include:

- **Conducting Market Analysis:** A detailed market analysis is essential for understanding the potential opportunities and risks associated with entering a new market. This analysis should cover factors such as market size, growth potential, competitive landscape, regulatory requirements, and customer preferences.

- **Tailoring Products and Services:** Companies should be prepared to tailor their products or services to meet the needs and preferences of customers in the new market. This may involve adapting pricing, packaging, or marketing strategies to align with local consumer behavior and expectations.

- **Building Local Partnerships:** Establishing partnerships with local distributors, suppliers, or service providers can help facilitate market entry and reduce the risk of operational challenges. Local partners can provide valuable insights into the market and help navigate regulatory and cultural complexities.

- **Scaling Internationally:** For companies expanding into international markets, additional considerations include managing currency risk, complying with international trade regulations, and establishing local legal entities. International expansion can be highly rewarding but requires careful planning and execution to ensure success.

Strategic Partnerships and Acquisitions

Strategic partnerships and acquisitions can play a key role in scaling the business by providing access to new markets, customers, and capabilities. Private equity firms often encourage their portfolio companies to pursue strategic partnerships and acquisitions as a way to accelerate growth and enhance competitive positioning.

1. Forming Strategic Partnerships

Strategic partnerships allow companies to leverage the strengths of other businesses to achieve mutual growth objectives. Partnerships can take many forms, including joint ventures, distribution agreements, co-marketing initiatives, or technology collaborations. The right partnership can help a company scale more quickly by providing access to new resources, expertise, and customer bases.

Benefits of strategic partnerships include:

- **Access to New Markets:** Partnering with a company that has an established presence in a target market can provide a faster, less risky way to enter that market. The partner's existing customer base, distribution network, or local knowledge can help accelerate growth.

- **Sharing Resources and Expertise:** Strategic partnerships allow companies to share resources, such as R&D capabilities, manufacturing facilities, or marketing channels, which can reduce costs and improve efficiency.

- **Enhancing Product Offerings:** Collaborating with a partner that offers complementary products or services can enhance the company's value proposition and increase cross-selling opportunities.

2. Pursuing Acquisitions

Acquisitions are a powerful growth strategy that allows companies to scale rapidly by acquiring new customers, technologies, or market share. Private equity firms are often experienced in managing mergers and acquisitions (M&A), and they may encourage their portfolio companies to pursue acquisitions as part of their scaling strategy.

Steps for executing a successful acquisition include:

- **Identifying Targets:** The first step in any acquisition is identifying potential targets that align with the company's strategic objectives. These targets could include competitors, companies with complementary products or services, or businesses in adjacent markets.

- **Conducting Due Diligence:** Before proceeding with an acquisition, it's critical to conduct thorough due diligence to assess the financial health, operational efficiency, and cultural fit of the target company. This ensures that the acquisition will deliver the desired benefits without introducing undue risk.

- **Integration Planning:** One of the most challenging aspects of an acquisition is integrating the target company into the existing organization. A detailed integration plan should be developed to ensure a smooth transition, including aligning systems, processes, and teams.

- **Maximizing Synergies:** The goal of any acquisition is to create value by leveraging synergies between the acquiring company and the target. These synergies could include cost savings, cross-selling opportunities, or operational efficiencies. By maximizing synergies, the company can accelerate growth and increase profitability.

Workshop Activities

Managing Growth Risks

Objective: Identify and mitigate risks associated with scaling a business.

Instructions:

- Build a scenario where a company is preparing for aggressive growth but faces potential risks (e.g., financial strain, supply chain disruptions, loss of quality control).

- Identify the top three risks associated with scaling the business and developing mitigation strategies for each risk.

- You should consider:

  » Financial risks, such as over-leveraging or inadequate cash flow to support growth.

  » Operational risks, such as bottlenecks in production or supply chain disruptions.

  » Customer satisfaction risks, such as quality control issues or delays in service delivery.

- Write out your risk mitigation strategies, explaining how they will address each risk and ensure sustainable growth.

Output: A risk mitigation plan that identifies the top risks associated with scaling and outlines specific strategies for managing those risks.

Actionable Takeaway: You will learn how to anticipate and mitigate the risks associated with scaling a business, ensuring that growth is managed sustainably and strategically.

Conclusion

Scaling a business is a multi-faceted process that requires strategic planning, operational efficiency, and the ability to seize new opportunities. Whether it's building and executing a scalable growth plan, expanding product lines, entering new markets, or forming strategic partnerships and acquisitions, companies must approach scaling with a disciplined, data-driven mindset. For private equity-backed companies, scaling is not just about growth–it's about creating value that drives a successful exit. By carefully crafting and executing a scaling strategy, companies can achieve sustainable growth, increase profitability, and deliver long-term success for both the business and its investors.

CHAPTER 11

Leveraging The PE Network

> *Leverage the power of the PE network to access resources, expertise, and partnerships that elevate your business beyond its boundaries.*

Private equity (PE) firms offer more than capital to their acquisitions—they provide a suite of resources, expertise, and connections that can drive growth, enhance efficiency, and achieve strategic goals. For portfolio companies, effectively leveraging the PE network is key to success. This includes accessing industry experts, operational insights, and collaboration with other portfolio companies. This chapter explores how to engage with the PE firm's resources and network, build relationships within the portfolio, and access new capital and specialized knowledge. Fully utilizing these opportunities can significantly improve operational efficiency, accelerate scaling, and boost financial performance.

How to Tap into PE
Resources and Expertise

One of the most significant advantages of being part of a private equity portfolio is the access to resources and expertise that the PE firm offers. PE firms employ highly experienced professionals with backgrounds in finance, operations, and strategy. They also have relationships with external consultants, industry specialists, and functional experts who can provide critical insights and help the company implement best practices. Learning how to tap into these resources is essential for maximizing the value of the PE relationship.

1. Leveraging Operational Expertise

Private equity firms typically employ seasoned operators and industry veterans who have extensive experience in optimizing business operations. These individuals are often tasked with working closely with portfolio companies to identify inefficiencies, streamline processes, and improve overall performance. By tapping into this expertise, portfolio companies can accelerate operationalinn improvements and achieve better results.

Key ways to leverage operational expertise include:

- **Engaging PE Operating Partners:** Many PE firms have operating partners or in-house operational teams whose sole focus is improving the performance of portfolio companies. These experts often have deep industry experience and can provide hands-on support in areas such as supply chain management, production optimization, or sales process improvements. Engaging with these operating partners early in the post-acquisition process can help the company identify quick wins and set the stage for long-term improvements.

- **Implementing Best Practices:** Private equity firms often have experience working with multiple companies across different industries. This gives them unique insights into best practices and operational benchmarks that can be applied to their portfolio companies. By adopting these best practices, companies can achieve higher levels of efficiency, reduce costs, and improve profitability.

- **Accessing Specialist Resources:** In addition to in-house experts, PE firms often have relationships with external consultants, advisors, and industry specialists who can provide targeted support in specific areas. Whether it's IT system upgrades, regulatory compliance, or marketing strategy, portfolio companies can leverage these external resources to solve complex challenges and drive growth.

2. Utilizing Financial Expertise and Support

Private equity firms are known for their financial acumen, and they provide valuable support to portfolio companies in areas such as capital structure optimization, financial reporting, and working capital management. Tapping into the PE firm's financial expertise can help portfolio companies improve cash flow, reduce debt, and strengthen their overall financial position.

Ways to leverage financial expertise include:

- **Capital Structure Optimization:** PE firms have extensive experience in optimizing capital structures to reduce the cost of capital, improve cash flow, and increase returns. They can help portfolio companies assess their debt levels, renegotiate loan terms, or raise additional equity to support growth initiatives. By working closely with the PE firm's financial team, companies can ensure that their capital structure is aligned with their growth strategy.

- **Improving Financial Reporting:** Accurate, timely financial reporting is critical for private equity firms, as they rely on data to make informed decisions about the performance of their portfolio companies. PE firms often implement standardized financial reporting systems that provide greater transparency and enable more effective decision-making. Portfolio companies can benefit from these systems by gaining better visibility into their financial performance and identifying areas for improvement.

- **Working Capital Management:** Efficient working capital management is essential for maintaining liquidity and funding day-to-day operations. PE firms can provide guidance on optimizing working capital by improving inventory management, accelerating receivables, or negotiating better payment terms with suppliers. By reducing the amount of cash tied up in working capital, companies can free up resources for growth and investment.

3. Strategic Guidance and Long-Term Planning

Private equity firms are highly focused on long-term value creation, and they provide strategic guidance to help portfolio companies achieve sustainable growth. This guidance often includes developing long-term business plans, identifying growth opportunities, and setting performance targets that align with the PE firm's investment thesis.

Key areas of strategic guidance include:

- **Developing Growth Strategies:** PE firms work closely with portfolio companies to identify and prioritize growth opportunities, such as entering new markets, expanding product lines, or pursuing strategic acquisitions. By leveraging the PE firm's expertise in scaling businesses, companies can develop more effective growth strategies that are aligned with their long-term goals.

- **Setting Performance Metrics:** To drive accountability and measure progress, PE firms often establish clear performance metrics (KPIs) for their portfolio companies. These metrics help ensure that the company is on track to meet its growth objectives and provide a framework for evaluating success. By setting measurable, data-driven goals, companies can stay focused on delivering results.

- **Exit Planning:** From the outset, private equity firms are thinking about the eventual exit strategy for the portfolio company. Whether the exit involves a sale to another company, an IPO, or another transaction, PE firms provide guidance on how to position the company for a successful exit. This may involve enhancing the company's financial performance, improving operational efficiency, or building a stronger market position.

Building Relationships with Portfolio Companies

In addition to leveraging the resources and expertise of the private equity firm itself, portfolio companies can benefit from building strong relationships with other companies in the PE firm's portfolio. These relationships create opportunities for collaboration, knowledge-sharing, and even joint ventures or partnerships that can drive growth and improve performance.

1. Creating a Portfolio Ecosystem

Many private equity firms view their portfolio companies as part of a broader ecosystem that can create synergies and drive mutual success. By fostering collaboration between portfolio companies, PE firms can unlock additional value and help companies achieve their growth objectives more efficiently.

Ways to create a portfolio ecosystem include:

- **Sharing Best Practices:** Portfolio companies often face similar challenges when it comes to scaling, operational improvements, and financial management. By sharing best practices and lessons learned, companies can accelerate their own growth and avoid common pitfalls. PE firms can facilitate these exchanges through portfolio-wide events, workshops, or webinars where companies can discuss their experiences and strategies.

- **Leveraging Shared Resources:** In some cases, portfolio companies can benefit from shared resources, such as access to centralized procurement, shared services (e.g., IT or HR), or group purchasing agreements. By pooling resources, companies can reduce costs, improve efficiency, and gain access to capabilities that they may not have been able to afford on their own.

- **Creating Cross-Selling Opportunities:** If portfolio companies operate in complementary industries or serve similar customer segments, there may be opportunities for cross-selling products or services. By collaborating on sales or marketing initiatives, companies can expand their customer base and generate additional revenue.

2. Networking and Relationship Building

Building relationships with other portfolio companies is not only about formal collaboration—it's also about networking and relationship building. Private equity firms often host networking events, conferences, or forums where executives from different portfolio companies can meet, exchange ideas, and build relationships. These networks can be invaluable sources of advice, support, and potential partnerships.

Key ways to network within the portfolio include:

- **Attending PE-Sponsored Events:** Many private equity firms host regular events, such as CEO summits, portfolio company conferences, or industry-specific forums, where leaders from across the portfolio can connect. These events provide an opportunity to share knowledge, discuss common challenges, and explore potential collaborations.

- **Building Peer Networks:** In addition to formal events, portfolio company leaders can build peer networks by reaching out to counterparts at other companies. These relationships can serve as informal advisory networks, where executives can seek advice on operational improvements, growth strategies, or other challenges they may be facing.

- **Exploring Joint Ventures or Partnerships:** In some cases, networking with other portfolio companies can lead to more formal partnerships, such as joint ventures or co-development initiatives. These partnerships can create synergies that help both companies grow more quickly and achieve their strategic objectives.

Gaining Access to New Capital and Expertise

One of the most significant benefits of being part of a private equity portfolio is the ability to access new capital and specialized expertise that may not have been available to the company before the acquisition. PE firms have extensive networks of investors, lenders, and industry experts, and they can provide portfolio companies with the resources they need to execute their growth strategies.

1. Accessing Additional Capital

Private equity firms have deep relationships with capital providers, including banks, institutional investors, and alternative lenders. This access to capital can be invaluable for portfolio companies that need funding to support growth initiatives, such as expanding into new markets, developing new products, or pursuing acquisitions.

Ways to access additional capital through the PE network include:

- **Debt Financing:** PE firms often have strong relationships with lenders who are willing to provide debt financing to portfolio companies at favorable terms. This could include traditional bank loans, mezzanine financing, or asset-based lending, depending on the company's needs and capital structure.

- **Equity Financing:** In some cases, the private equity firm itself may be willing to provide additional equity financing to support the company's growth. Alternatively, the PE firm may introduce the company to co-investors who can provide additional capital in exchange for an equity stake.

- **Strategic Investors:** PE firms also have relationships with strategic investors, such as corporate venture arms or industry-specific investment funds, that may be interested in investing in portfolio companies. These investors can provide not only capital but also industry expertise and strategic guidance.

2. Gaining Access to Specialized Expertise

In addition to capital, private equity firms can provide portfolio companies with access to specialized expertise that can accelerate growth and improve performance. This expertise may come in the form of industry-specific advisors, functional experts, or external consultants who can provide targeted support in key areas.

Examples of specialized expertise include:

- **Industry Advisors:** Many PE firms have relationships with industry experts who can provide insights into market trends, competitive dynamics, and customer behavior. These advisors can help portfolio companies refine their strategies and identify new growth opportunities.

- **Functional Experts:** Private equity firms often employ or have access to functional experts in areas such as sales, marketing, IT, or human resources. These experts can provide hands-on support in optimizing key functions, implementing best practices, and improving overall performance.

- **External Consultants:** In some cases, PE firms may engage external consultants to provide specialized support for portfolio companies. This could include consulting firms that specialize in operational improvements, M&A advisory, or digital transformation. By leveraging these external resources, companies can access the expertise they need to overcome specific challenges and drive growth.

Workshop Activities

Identifying and Building Strategic Relationships

Objective: Explore strategies for building and maintaining strong relationships with other portfolio companies and key stakeholders within the private equity network.

Instructions:

- Develop a fictional scenario where their company is seeking to build relationships with other portfolio companies to share best practices, leverage joint resources, or explore cross-company collaborations.

- Identify potential portfolio companies that would benefit from a strategic relationship and developing a plan for initiating and building these relationships by:

  » Establishing clear mutual benefits (e.g., joint marketing efforts, shared technology, or supply chain efficiencies).

  » Identifying key stakeholders within the PE firm and portfolio companies to approach.

  » Outlining specific steps to build and maintain these relationships over time (e.g., regular meetings, collaboration platforms, or joint projects).

- Write our your relationship-building plan, explaining how these relationships will create value for both companies.

Output: A strategic relationship-building plan that outlines potential partnerships with portfolio companies and key stakeholders, along with actionable steps to foster collaboration.

Actionable Takeaway: You will gain experience in building and nurturing strategic relationships within the PE network, learning how to create win-win scenarios for all parties involved.

Conclusion

Leveraging the private equity network is one of the most powerful tools available to portfolio companies. By tapping into the resources, expertise, and relationships provided by the PE firm, companies can accelerate their growth, improve operational efficiency, and achieve their strategic objectives more effectively. Whether it's accessing financial expertise, building relationships with other portfolio companies, or gaining access to new capital and specialized knowledge, the private equity network offers a wealth of opportunities for companies that know how to take advantage of it. For portfolio companies, building strong relationships within the PE ecosystem and proactively seeking out support can lead to long-term success and maximize the value of the private equity investment.

CHAPTER 12

Innovating Under New Ownership

> ""
>
> *True innovation thrives in a culture that embraces change, encourages disruptive thinking, and is fueled by data and creativity.*
>
> ""

Innovation is crucial for the long-term growth and competitiveness of any business, including those acquired by private equity (PE). While PE focuses on operational efficiency and cost reductions, maintaining innovation is essential for sustainable value creation. Balancing the short-term financial goals of PE owners with the long-term need for market competitiveness poses a challenge. This chapter will discuss how to adapt research and development (R&D) and innovation cycles under PE ownership, use data and analytics for smarter innovation, and incorporate disruptive thinking into growth strategies. Recognizing innovation's role in long-term growth, many PE firms encourage ongoing investment in innovative approaches.

Rethinking R&D and Innovation Cycles

Innovation is often viewed as a long-term investment, requiring significant resources and patience before new products, services, or processes deliver tangible results. However, under private equity ownership, the pressure to deliver returns within a specific investment horizon can create tension with traditional R&D timelines. Companies must rethink their approach to R&D to ensure that innovation continues to thrive while meeting the PE firm's expectations for measurable outcomes.

1. Aligning R&D with Strategic Priorities

In a private equity environment, R&D investments must be closely aligned with the company's strategic priorities and growth objectives. Unlike large, diversified corporations that can afford to take risks on multiple R&D initiatives, PE-backed companies often have more focused goals. As a result, it's essential to prioritize innovation projects that have a clear line of sight to the company's core competencies and market opportunities.

Steps to align R&D with strategic priorities:

- **Focus on High-Impact Projects:** Private equity firms typically want to see quick, tangible returns on R&D investments. Companies should focus on projects that have the potential to generate significant revenue or improve operational efficiency in the near term. These projects might include incremental innovations that enhance existing products or services or new technologies that address a specific customer pain point.

- **Create a Clear Innovation Roadmap:** Developing an innovation roadmap that outlines the company's short-term and long-term R&D priorities can help ensure that innovation efforts are aligned with business objectives. This roadmap should be regularly updated to reflect changes in the market, customer needs, and technological advancements.

- **Measure Innovation ROI:** To meet the expectations of PE owners, companies must be able to demonstrate the value of their R&D efforts. This requires implementing metrics to measure the return on investment (ROI) for innovation initiatives. Metrics might include the revenue generated from new products, cost savings from process improvements, or market share gained through innovation.

2. Accelerating Innovation Cycles

Traditional R&D cycles can take years to deliver results, but private equity firms often operate on a much shorter timeline, expecting measurable outcomes within three to seven years. To address this challenge, companies must find ways to accelerate their innovation cycles without sacrificing quality or risking long-term competitiveness.

Strategies for accelerating innovation cycles include:

- **Agile R&D Processes:** Adopting agile methodologies in R&D can help companies bring new products and services to market faster. Agile innovation involves breaking down large projects into smaller, manageable phases, testing and iterating rapidly, and making adjustments based on real-time feedback. This approach allows companies to reduce the time it takes to move from concept to commercialization.

- **Collaborative Innovation:** Partnering with external organizations, such as universities, research institutions, or technology startups, can help speed up the R&D process. By collaborating with external experts or leveraging existing technologies, companies can reduce the time and resources required to develop new innovations.

- **Pilot Programs and Prototyping:** Testing new products or services through pilot programs or rapid prototyping allows companies to validate ideas quickly and gather feedback before scaling up. This iterative approach can help avoid costly mistakes and ensure that the company is investing in innovation projects with the highest likelihood of success.

3. Balancing Short-Term and Long-Term Innovation Goals

Under private equity ownership, the pressure to deliver short-term financial results can sometimes lead to a focus on incremental innovations rather than more transformative, long-term projects. While incremental innovations are valuable, companies must also invest in disruptive, long-term innovation to remain competitive in the future.

Balancing short-term and long-term innovation goals involves:

- **Creating an Innovation Portfolio:** Just as companies diversify their financial investments, they should also diversify their innovation efforts. This means maintaining a portfolio of innovation projects that includes both short-term, incremental improvements and long-term, transformative initiatives. By balancing these two types of innovation, companies can meet short-term financial goals while laying the foundation for future growth.

- **Setting Innovation Milestones:** To manage the tension between short-term and long-term goals, companies should set clear milestones for innovation projects. These milestones help track progress and ensure that even long-term initiatives are delivering value along the way. Regularly reviewing these milestones with the PE firm can help maintain alignment and demonstrate the ongoing value of innovation efforts.

Driving Innovation Through
Data and Analytics

In today's data-driven world, companies have more information at their fingertips than ever before, and leveraging this data is key to driving smarter, more efficient innovation. Private equity firms understand the power of data and often encourage their portfolio companies to adopt data analytics tools and technologies that can help improve decision-making and accelerate the innovation process.

1. Using Data to Identify Innovation Opportunities

Data analytics can provide valuable insights into customer behavior, market trends, and operational performance, helping companies identify new innovation opportunities that are grounded in real-world needs. By analyzing data from multiple sources—such as customer feedback, sales patterns, and competitive intelligence—companies can make more informed decisions about where to focus their innovation efforts.

Examples of how data can drive innovation:

- **Customer Insights:** Analyzing customer data, such as purchasing habits, preferences, and feedback, can help companies identify unmet needs and develop new products or services to address those needs. For example, if customer data shows a growing demand for sustainability, the company might prioritize eco-friendly product innovations.

- **Market Trends:** Data analytics tools can help companies track industry trends and stay ahead of emerging market shifts. By using predictive analytics, companies can anticipate future demand and position themselves to capitalize on new opportunities before competitors do.

- **Operational Data:** Data from internal operations, such as production efficiency or supply chain performance, can be used to identify areas for process innovation. For instance, if data reveals bottlenecks in the manufacturing process, the company can explore new technologies or methods to improve efficiency and reduce costs.

2. Leveraging Predictive Analytics for Smarter Innovation

Predictive analytics takes data analysis a step further by using historical data to forecast future trends, behaviors, and outcomes. This capability can be particularly valuable for innovation, as it allows companies to anticipate changes in the market and customer needs, enabling them to develop solutions proactively.

How predictive analytics supports innovation:

- **Anticipating Customer Demand:** Predictive analytics can help companies forecast future customer demand based on historical purchasing data, economic indicators, and market conditions. This allows companies to innovate ahead of demand, ensuring that they are ready to meet customer needs when new trends emerge.

- **Reducing R&D Risk:** Innovation is inherently risky, but predictive analytics can help reduce some of that risk by providing data-driven insights into the likelihood of success for new products or services. By analyzing factors such as market size, customer adoption rates, and competitive dynamics, companies can make more informed decisions about which innovation projects to pursue.

- **Optimizing Product Development:** Predictive analytics can also help companies optimize the product development process by identifying potential issues before they become costly problems. For example, predictive maintenance algorithms can be used to identify potential equipment failures during the manufacturing process, allowing companies to address issues before they impact production.

3. Building a Data-Driven Culture of Innovation

To fully leverage the power of data and analytics for innovation, companies must build a culture that prioritizes data-driven decision-making. This involves ensuring that employees at all levels have access to the data they need, are trained in how to interpret and use that data, and are encouraged to experiment and take calculated risks based on data insights.

Key elements of a data-driven innovation culture:

- **Investing in Data Infrastructure:** To drive innovation through data, companies need the right tools and infrastructure in place. This includes investing in data analytics platforms, business intelligence tools, and cloud-based systems that allow employees to access and analyze data in real-time.

- **Encouraging Experimentation:** Data-driven innovation requires a willingness to experiment and iterate. Companies should create an environment where employees feel empowered to use data to test new ideas, even if those ideas may not always lead to immediate success. By fostering a culture of experimentation, companies can accelerate the innovation process and uncover new opportunities.

- **Cross-Functional Collaboration:** Innovation is often most successful when it involves collaboration across different departments, such as R&D, marketing, and operations. By breaking down silos and encouraging cross-functional teams to work together and share data, companies can drive more holistic, integrated innovation efforts.

How PE Encourages Disruptive Thinking

While private equity firms are known for their focus on financial performance and operational efficiency, many also recognize the value of disruptive thinking in driving long-term growth. Disruptive innovation involves challenging the status quo, embracing new technologies, and rethinking traditional business models to create breakthroughs that can redefine markets and industries. PE firms can play an important role in fostering a culture of disruptive thinking within their portfolio companies.

1. Encouraging a "Challenge the Status Quo" Mentality

Private equity firms often bring a fresh perspective to the companies they acquire, and they encourage portfolio companies to challenge established norms and rethink traditional ways of doing business. This disruptive mindset can lead to breakthrough innovations that give the company a competitive edge.

Ways PE firms encourage disruptive thinking:

- **Questioning Assumptions:** PE firms are not tied to the company's legacy practices, which allows them to challenge long-held assumptions about how the business should operate. By encouraging employees to question the status quo and explore new ways of solving problems, PE firms can foster a culture of disruptive innovation.

- **Risk-Taking and Experimentation:** While PE firms expect results, they also understand that innovation requires taking calculated risks. Encouraging experimentation–whether through pilot programs, rapid prototyping, or beta testing–allows companies to test disruptive ideas in a controlled environment. If an idea proves successful, it can be scaled; if not, the company can learn from the failure and move on.

- **Empowering Intrapreneurs:** Some of the best disruptive innovations come from within the company itself, driven by employees who think like entrepreneurs ("intrapreneurs"). PE firms can support intrapreneurship by creating innovation labs, offering internal grants for disruptive projects, or encouraging employees to pitch new ideas directly to leadership.

2. Leveraging Emerging Technologies

Private equity firms often push their portfolio companies to adopt new technologies that can disrupt traditional business models or create new revenue streams. Whether it's artificial intelligence (AI), machine learning, blockchain, or the Internet of Things (IoT), emerging technologies offer opportunities for companies to innovate in ways that were previously unimaginable.

Examples of leveraging emerging technologies for disruptive innovation:

- AI and Automation: AI-powered automation can revolutionize business processes, from customer service and supply chain management to data analysis and decision-making. By automating repetitive tasks, companies can free up resources to focus on higher-value innovation efforts.

- Blockchain Technology: Blockchain has the potential to disrupt industries by providing a secure, transparent way to manage transactions, data, and contracts. Companies that embrace blockchain for applications such as supply chain tracking, digital identity verification, or decentralized finance can position themselves as industry leaders in innovation.

- IoT and Smart Devices: The Internet of Things (IoT) allows companies to create connected devices that collect and transmit data, enabling new business models and customer experiences. For example, companies in manufacturing, healthcare, or transportation can use IoT devices to monitor performance, predict maintenance needs, and optimize operations.

3. Driving Industry Disruption Through Acquisitions and Partnerships

Private equity firms often encourage their portfolio companies to pursue disruptive innovation through strategic acquisitions or partnerships. By acquiring startups or partnering with emerging technology companies, portfolio companies can gain access to new capabilities, intellectual property, or disruptive business models that allow them to lead industry transformation.

Key strategies for driving disruption through M&A and partnerships:

- **Acquiring Disruptive Startups:** Acquiring innovative startups that are developing disruptive technologies or business models can help portfolio companies stay ahead of industry trends. These acquisitions provide access to new talent, intellectual property, and technologies that can accelerate the company's own innovation efforts.

- **Forming Strategic Partnerships:** In some cases, forming strategic partnerships with disruptive companies can provide similar benefits to acquisitions without the need for a full-scale purchase. By collaborating with technology companies, research institutions, or industry disruptors, portfolio companies can gain access to cutting-edge innovations and stay ahead of competitors.

- **Expanding into New Markets:** Disruptive innovation often involves entering new markets or creating entirely new categories. PE-backed companies that are willing to take bold steps and explore new markets can position themselves as leaders in emerging industries.

Encouraging Disruptive Thinking

Objective: Develop strategies for encouraging disruptive thinking and fostering a culture of innovation within the organization post-acquisition.

Instructions:

- Provide participants with a fictional company that is struggling to innovate in a competitive market. The new private equity owners are encouraging disruptive thinking to shake up the industry and lead to breakthrough innovations.

- Develop a plan to encourage disruptive thinking within the company by:

  » Identifying barriers to innovation and disruptive thinking (e.g., risk aversion, rigid processes, lack of resources).

  » Proposing initiatives to encourage out-of-the-box thinking, such as innovation sprints, brainstorming sessions, or cross-functional collaboration.

  » Creating a culture that rewards experimentation and embraces calculated risks.

- Write out your disruptive thinking plan, explaining how you will foster a culture of innovation that encourages employees to think beyond the status quo.

Output: A disruptive thinking plan that outlines specific actions the company will take to foster a culture of innovation and encourage employees to explore breakthrough ideas.

Actionable Takeaway: You will learn how to remove barriers to innovation and create an environment where disruptive thinking is encouraged and rewarded, leading to breakthrough ideas and products.

Conclusion

Innovation under private equity ownership requires a delicate balance between meeting the short-term performance expectations of the new owners and driving long-term, disruptive growth. By rethinking R&D and innovation cycles, leveraging data and analytics, and fostering a culture of disruptive thinking, companies can continue to innovate and stay competitive in a rapidly changing market. Private equity firms understand that innovation is key to creating long-term value, and they are often willing to invest in forward-thinking strategies that drive growth and transform industries. For portfolio companies, embracing innovation under new ownership is not only a path to success but a necessity for staying relevant in an increasingly competitive landscape.

CHAPTER 13

Dealing with Difficult People

> ❝
>
> *Navigating difficult personalities with empathy and strategy transforms conflicts into opportunities for collaboration and growth.*
>
> ❞

In every business environment, dealing with difficult people is inevitable. Whether it's a colleague who consistently complains, an aggressive team member who dominates discussions, or a passive-aggressive coworker who resists collaboration, challenging behaviors can disrupt workflows and harm morale. However, with the right strategies, you can manage these interactions constructively and maintain a productive, respectful work environment.

This chapter equips you with practical tools to recognize difficult behaviors, understand their root causes, and respond effectively, turning potential conflicts into opportunities for collaboration and growth.

Recognizing Common Types of Difficult People

1. The Complainer

- **Behavior:** Frequently expresses dissatisfaction about processes, tasks, or coworkers but rarely offers solutions.

- **Example:** A team member consistently complains about deadlines but doesn't take proactive steps to manage their time.

Strategy: Acknowledge their concerns without indulging negativity. Ask solution-oriented questions like, *"What would help you manage this deadline better?"*

2. The Aggressor

- **Behavior:** Uses intimidation, dominating conversations, or dismissing others' ideas.

- **Example:** A coworker who consistently interrupts in meetings, shutting down others' contributions.

Strategy: Remain calm and assertive. Use neutral language to redirect the conversation: *"I value everyone's input. Let's hear other perspectives before moving forward."*

3. The Passive-Aggressive

- **Behavior:** Avoids direct confrontation but undermines progress with subtle resistance or sabotage.

- **Example:** A colleague who agrees to take on a task but

delays it intentionally, affecting the team's workflow.

> **Strategy:** Address the behavior directly and diplomatically: *"I noticed the task hasn't been completed. Is there something preventing you from finishing it?"*

4. The Procrastinator

- **Behavior:** Consistently delays tasks, often leaving others to pick up the slack.

- **Example:** A team member who habitually misses deadlines, causing bottlenecks in the project.

> **Strategy:** Set clear deadlines and follow up with reminders. Offer to break tasks into smaller, manageable steps.

Understanding Root Causes

People often exhibit difficult behaviors for deeper reasons:

- **Stress or Overload:** A person may act out because they feel overwhelmed or unsupported.

- **Unclear Expectations:** Misunderstandings about roles or goals can lead to frustration or disengagement.

- **Lack of Skills:** Some behaviors stem from an individual's inability to manage conflict or work collaboratively.

- **Personality Differences:** Natural differences in communication or working styles can sometimes cause friction.

By understanding the root causes, you can address behaviors with empathy and focus on solutions rather than assigning blame.

Strategies for Managing Difficult People

1. Stay Calm and Composed

Responding emotionally to difficult behaviors often escalates conflict. Practice deep breathing or take a moment to think before responding.

2. Use Active Listening

Show that you are genuinely hearing their concerns. Restate their points to ensure understanding: *"I hear that you're frustrated about the timeline. Let's discuss how we can address that."*

3. Set Boundaries

Politely but firmly establish limits. For example: *"I'm happy to discuss this during work hours, but let's focus on our current priorities."*

4. Be Solution-Oriented

Shift the focus from problems to solutions. For instance: *"What changes can we make to avoid this issue moving forward?"*

5. Document Interactions

If behavior persists, keep records of problematic incidents, especially if they impact performance or team dynamics. This documentation can be helpful if escalation is needed.

Examples in Action

1. **Scenario:** A passive-aggressive colleague consistently misses meeting deadlines.

   Solution: Approach them in a private conversation. Use "I" statements: *"I noticed the report wasn't submitted on time, which affected the team's progress. Is there something preventing you from completing it on schedule?"*

2. **Scenario:** An aggressive coworker frequently interrupts in meetings.

   Solution: During the meeting, calmly say, *"I appreciate your enthusiasm. Let's ensure everyone has a chance to contribute before we move forward."*

3. **Scenario:** A complainer continually criticizes new processes.

   Solution: Redirect their negativity by involving them in solutions: *"What steps do you think we can take to improve the process?"*

Workshop Activities

Activity 1: Role-Playing Difficult Behaviors

Objective: Practice responding to different types of difficult behaviors in a safe and controlled environment.

Instructions:

1. Divide participants into pairs. Assign one person to play a "difficult person" (e.g., complainer, aggressor) and the other to respond constructively.
2. Provide scenarios for role-playing (e.g., a team member consistently interrupts during meetings).
3. After 5 minutes, switch roles.

Debrief: Discuss what strategies worked and how participants felt during the interactions.

Activity 2: Identifying Root Causes

Objective: Develop empathy by exploring potential reasons behind difficult behaviors.

Instructions:

1. Provide participants with challenging behavior scenarios.
2. Ask them to brainstorm potential root causes (e.g., stress, unclear expectations).
3. Discuss how understanding these causes can shape their approach to resolution.

Activity 3: Building a Response Toolkit

Objective: Create personalized strategies for handling difficult behaviors.

Instructions:

1. Ask participants to list 2-3 challenging behaviors they've encountered in their work.

2. For each behavior, develop a script or plan for responding constructively.

3. Share examples with the group for feedback.

Activity 4: Boundary-Setting Practice

Objective: Practice establishing professional boundaries with difficult people.

Instructions:

1. Provide scenarios where participants must set boundaries (e.g., a colleague tries to shift their workload onto others).

2. Ask participants to write and practice a polite but firm response.

3. Discuss how to maintain these boundaries without escalating conflict.

Conclusion

By understanding and addressing difficult behaviors, you can turn potential conflicts into opportunities for collaboration and personal growth. Practicing these strategies will not only improve your work environment but also enhance your leadership and interpersonal skills.

CHAPTER 14

Helping People Make Decisions

"

Empower others to decide by providing clarity, simplifying choices, and fostering confidence in their judgment.

"

In business, the ability to make decisions quickly and effectively is a crucial skill that drives progress and innovation. However, not everyone finds decision-making easy. Colleagues, subordinates, or even leaders may struggle with hesitation, overthinking, or fear of failure. This chapter explores strategies for guiding and empowering others to make confident decisions, reducing delays and ensuring that momentum is maintained in the organization.

Helping others make decisions is not about taking control but rather providing support, clarity, and structure. By mastering this skill, you can foster a collaborative and results-driven environment.

Why People Struggle to Make Decisions

Before diving into strategies, it's essential to understand the common reasons behind decision-making challenges:

1. Fear of Failure:

Example: A team member hesitates to propose a new vendor, fearing it might reflect poorly if the vendor underperforms.

Solution: Normalize failure as part of growth. Remind them that every decision offers valuable lessons.

2. Overwhelmed by Options (Analysis Paralysis):

Example: A project leader delays picking a design because they're paralyzed by the sheer number of choices.

Solution: Help narrow options to the top two or three and focus on the most impactful factors.

3. Unclear Priorities:

Example: A colleague avoids deciding on a marketing strategy because they're unsure of the company's main goals.

Solution: Clarify the objectives and how the decision aligns with them.

4. Fear of Accountability:

Example: A manager avoids committing to a restructuring plan, worried they'll face blame if it fails.

> **Solution:** Share responsibility and emphasize team collaboration in achieving outcomes.

Strategies for Helping People Make Decisions

1. Provide Context and Clarity

People make better decisions when they understand the broader context. Share relevant information and clarify the decision's purpose.

> **Example:** *"This decision will shape our product launch timeline, so let's focus on what's achievable by Q2."*

2. Simplify the Choices

Reduce complexity by narrowing down options. Too many choices can be overwhelming, so focus on the top contenders.

> **Example:** *"Here are three potential marketing channels. Based on our budget, I recommend focusing on A and B."*

3. Use Decision-Making Frameworks

Tools like pros and cons lists, decision trees, or cost-benefit analyses can structure the process.

> **Example:** *"Let's list the advantages and risks of each option to see which aligns best with our goals."*

4. Set Clear Deadlines

Indecision thrives in open-ended timelines. Assign realistic but firm deadlines to create a sense of urgency.

Example: *"Let's finalize our vendor selection by next Friday so we can stay on schedule."*

5. Encourage Collaborative Decision-Making

Involve others in the process to share perspectives and reduce the pressure on one individual.

Example: *"Let's brainstorm as a team to identify the best strategy and then decide together."*

6. Build Confidence Through Support

Encourage decision-makers by validating their expertise and offering reassurance.

Example: *"You've handled similar challenges before and succeeded. I trust your judgment on this."*

7. Focus on Actionable Steps

Break decisions into smaller, more manageable parts to reduce overwhelm.

Example: *"Today, let's decide on the design elements. Next week, we'll tackle the pricing model."*

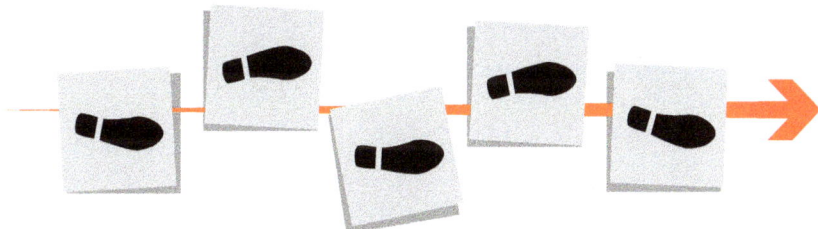

Examples in Action

1. **Scenario: A team member struggles to choose between two potential suppliers.**

   Solution: Provide a comparison of the suppliers' strengths and weaknesses. Use a cost-benefit analysis to guide the decision: *"Supplier A is slightly more expensive but offers better delivery reliability."*

2. **Scenario: A manager is hesitant to approve a hiring decision.**

   Solution: Reframe the decision as an opportunity: *"Bringing this person on board could address our staffing bottlenecks. Let's set a 90-day evaluation period to assess their fit."*

3. **Scenario: A colleague delays launching a new initiative.**

   Solution: Narrow the decision to the next actionable step: *"Let's focus on selecting the pilot location first, and we can evaluate results before scaling."*

Workshop Activities

Activity 1: Decision-Making Framework Practice

Objective: Learn to apply decision-making frameworks to real-world scenarios.

Instructions:

1. Provide participants with a scenario (e.g., selecting a

new software system).

2. Have them use a framework like a pros and cons list, a decision tree, or a risk-reward matrix to analyze the options.

3. Share their decision-making process and final recommendation with the group.

Debrief: Discuss how using frameworks made the process clearer and more actionable.

Activity 2: Collaborative Decision Simulation

Objective: Practice collaborative decision-making in a group setting.

Instructions:

1. Divide participants into teams and give them a scenario requiring a group decision (e.g., allocating a limited marketing budget).

2. Teams must work together to evaluate options and make a decision within a set timeframe.

3. Each team presents their decision and rationale to the larger group.

Debrief: Highlight the benefits of collaboration in reducing pressure and generating diverse perspectives.

Activity 3: Role-Playing Confidence Building

Objective: Practice supporting someone hesitant to make a decision.

Instructions:

1. Pair participants. One plays the indecisive person,

and the other plays a supportive colleague or leader.

2. Provide a scenario (e.g., deciding on a project timeline). The "supporter" uses validation and structured guidance to help the other make a decision.

3. Switch roles and repeat with a new scenario.

Debrief: Discuss how confidence-building techniques influenced the decision-making process.

Activity 4: Breaking Down Big Decisions

Objective: Practice simplifying complex decisions into smaller, actionable steps.

Instructions:

1. Provide participants with a challenging decision (e.g., launching a new product line).

2. Have them break the decision into smaller, time-bound steps (e.g., conducting market research, setting pricing, finalizing launch date).

3. Share their step-by-step plans with the group.

Debrief: Discuss how breaking down decisions reduces overwhelm and builds momentum.

Conclusion

Helping others make decisions is a collaborative and empowering process. By providing clarity, simplifying choices, and offering support, you can foster confidence and momentum in your team. Practicing these strategies will ensure better outcomes and stronger relationships, making decision-making a shared strength across your organization.

THE EXIT STRATEGY AND BEYOND

The culmination of a private equity (PE) investment is the exit strategy, the moment when the PE firm realizes the returns on its investment by selling the company, merging it with another entity, or taking it public through an initial public offering (IPO). However, the exit is more than just a financial transaction; it represents a major transition for the company and its employees. The way the company is positioned and prepared for this event is crucial for ensuring a smooth transition, sustained growth, and long-term success.

In this section, we will explore the various exit strategies that PE firms employ, from IPOs to mergers and sales, and discuss how companies can be strategically prepared for these transitions. We will examine the operational, financial, and cultural changes that must be managed to ensure the company is positioned for an optimal outcome. Most importantly, we will address how to guide management and employees through this often uncertain period, ensuring that morale stays high and that the business is set up to succeed long after the PE firm has exited.

CHAPTER 15

Preparing for The Next Exit

"

A well-planned exit is the ultimate act of strategic foresight, positioning your company for future success and sustainability.

"

Private equity (PE) ownership is inherently temporary, with the end goal being to maximize investment value through an exit strategy. The duration a PE firm holds a portfolio company can vary, but as the company approaches its exit phase—whether through a sale, merger, or IPO—management and employees must navigate a critical transition. This requires strategic planning and positioning to ensure success. This chapter will examine various PE exit strategies, offer guidance on preparing the company for a successful exit, and discuss how to ready management and employees for upcoming changes, impacting the company's future success.

Understanding the PE Exit Strategy: IPO, Sale, or Merger

The exit strategy is the final phase of the PE investment lifecycle, and it typically involves one of three primary routes: a sale to another company (either strategic or financial), a merger, or an IPO. Each of these exit options comes with distinct financial, operational, and regulatory implications for the company. Understanding these options is key to preparing the company for the next phase.

1. Initial Public Offering (IPO)

An IPO is one of the most prestigious and high-profile exit strategies available, where the private equity firm takes the company public by offering its shares on a stock exchange. While this option allows the PE firm to unlock significant value from the investment, it also subjects the company to increased regulatory scrutiny, transparency, and governance requirements.

Key considerations for an IPO include:

- **Regulatory Compliance:** Going public requires strict adherence to regulatory standards, including the filing of detailed financial disclosures, adhering to governance requirements, and meeting reporting deadlines. The company must have well-established financial controls, accurate reporting systems, and legal compliance in place to successfully navigate this process.

- **Investor Relations:** Once the company is public, it is

accountable to shareholders and analysts. Building a strong investor relations strategy is critical to communicating the company's vision and performance and maintaining investor confidence.

- **Operational Readiness:** An IPO signals that the company is ready to operate under the public market's pressures, which include the ability to scale quickly, maintain profitability, and deliver consistent financial performance. Private equity firms often prepare portfolio companies for an IPO by focusing on growth, profitability, and operational efficiency well before the IPO process begins.

While an IPO can be highly lucrative, it is also a lengthy and complex process that may not be the right choice for every company.

2. Sale to a Strategic Buyer

A sale to a strategic buyer involves selling the company to another company, usually within the same or a related industry, that sees value in the portfolio company's products, services, or market position. Strategic buyers are typically motivated by the potential synergies they can realize through the acquisition, such as expanded market share, complementary technologies, or cost savings.

Key considerations for a strategic sale include:

- **Synergy Potential:** The company must be positioned as an attractive acquisition target for a strategic buyer by highlighting potential synergies. These synergies could come from combining operations, leveraging each company's customer base, or integrating complementary products or services.

- **Cultural Fit:** In a strategic sale, the cultural integration of the two companies is critical. If the cultures are not compatible, the success of the merger or acquisition could be jeopardized. It is important to assess cultural alignment and ensure a smooth integration process post-sale.

- **Market Positioning:** Strategic buyers are often interested in acquiring companies that offer something they cannot build or replicate on their own. Companies preparing for a strategic sale must emphasize their unique competitive advantages, whether it's intellectual property, market dominance, or specialized expertise.

3. Sale to a Financial Buyer

A sale to a financial buyer, such as another private equity firm, is another common exit strategy. In this case, the financial buyer is looking for a company that has growth potential, operational improvements, or other opportunities for value creation. A financial sale is typically less focused on synergies and more on the company's standalone value and future potential for growth.

Key considerations for a financial sale include:

- **Financial Performance:** A financial buyer will closely scrutinize the company's historical financial performance, including revenue growth, profitability (EBITDA), and cash flow. It's essential to demonstrate a strong financial track record and the ability to continue generating returns.

- **Scalability:** Financial buyers are often looking for companies that can be scaled further, whether through geographic expansion, product line extensions, or operational improvements. Companies preparing for a financial sale should have a clear growth plan that outlines how the business can be scaled after the acquisition.

- **Exit Strategy for the New Owner:** Financial buyers, particularly other PE firms, will be looking ahead to their own exit strategy. Companies can position themselves as attractive targets by demonstrating how value can continue to be created over the next three to five years.

4. Merger with Another Company

A merger is another potential exit route, where the portfolio company merges with another company to create a larger, more competitive entity. Mergers are often pursued when there are complementary strengths between the two companies that can drive higher growth or cost efficiencies.

Key considerations for a merger include:

- **Synergies and Integration:** As with a strategic sale, synergies are a major driver of value in a merger. The company must be able to demonstrate how the merger will lead to cost savings, increased market share, or enhanced operational efficiency.

- **Cultural and Operational Integration:** Mergers can be complex due to the need to integrate not only operations but also company cultures. Ensuring that both companies are aligned on their strategic vision, values, and operational processes is critical to a successful merger.

- **Regulatory Approval:** Some mergers, particularly those involving large companies or companies in regulated industries, may require regulatory approval. It's important to assess any potential regulatory hurdles early in the process.

How to Position the Company

for a Successful Exit

Positioning the company for a successful exit, regardless of the exit strategy, requires careful preparation in several key areas. Private equity firms often start preparing for the exit years in advance, focusing on improving financial performance, strengthening market positioning, and ensuring operational excellence. These efforts are designed to make the company an attractive target for buyers or investors and maximize the value realized at exit.

1. Strengthening Financial Performance

One of the most critical aspects of preparing for an exit is ensuring that the company's financial performance is strong and consistent. Potential buyers or investors will scrutinize the company's financials, looking for evidence of sustainable growth, profitability, and cash flow.

Steps to strengthen financial performance include:

- **Focus on EBITDA and Margins:** Earnings before interest, taxes, depreciation, and amortization (EBITDA) is a key metric for potential buyers. Private equity firms often work to improve EBITDA by reducing costs, increasing operational efficiency, and focusing on higher-margin products or services.

- **Optimizing Cash Flow:** Healthy cash flow is essential for attracting buyers. Companies should focus on improving working capital management, reducing debt, and ensuring that cash flow remains strong even as the company grows.

- **Demonstrating Revenue Growth:** Buyers want to see a strong growth trajectory. Companies preparing for an exit should focus on driving top-line revenue growth through new customer acquisition, market expansion, or product innovation.

2. Enhancing Market Position

A company's market position plays a critical role in its attractiveness to potential buyers or investors. Companies that are leaders in their industry, have a strong brand, or possess a unique competitive advantage are more likely to command higher valuations.

Ways to enhance market position include:

- **Building a Strong Brand:** Companies with strong brand recognition and customer loyalty are more attractive to buyers. Investing in brand development, customer satisfaction, and marketing can help strengthen the company's market position.

- **Differentiation Through Innovation:** Companies that offer unique products, services, or technologies are more likely to attract strategic buyers. Continuing to invest in innovation and R&D can help differentiate the company from competitors.

- **Expanding Market Share:** Increasing market share through organic growth or acquisitions can enhance the company's value. Buyers are often willing to pay a premium for companies that dominate their market or have significant growth potential in underserved markets.

3. Operational Efficiency and Scalability

Operational excellence is another critical factor that buyers consider when evaluating a company. Companies that have efficient, scalable operations are more likely to succeed post-acquisition, making them more attractive to buyers.

Steps to improve operational efficiency and scalability include:

- **Streamlining Processes:** Private equity firms often focus on process optimization to reduce costs and improve efficiency. Ensuring that the company's operations are lean, standardized, and scalable is critical to positioning the company for a successful exit.

- **Leveraging Technology:** Implementing technology solutions that improve efficiency, enhance customer experiences, and enable scalability can increase the company's value. Buyers will look for companies that are using technology to drive innovation and operational improvements.

- **Building a Strong Leadership Team:** A capable and experienced leadership team is essential for ensuring the company's success post-exit. Buyers want to know that the company has a team in place that can continue to drive growth and operational excellence after the transition.

Preparing Management and Employees for Another Transition

Exiting private equity ownership can be a period of uncertainty for management and employees. The company may be sold to a new owner, merge with another entity, or become a publicly traded company, each of which brings its own challenges. Preparing the workforce for another transition is essential for maintaining morale, retaining key talent, and ensuring operational continuity.

1. Communicating the Exit Plan

Clear and transparent communication is critical during the exit phase. Employees and management need to understand the exit strategy, the timeline, and what to expect during the transition.

Best practices for communication include:

- **Regular Updates:** Providing regular updates on the status of the exit process can help alleviate uncertainty and prevent rumors from spreading. Leadership should communicate key milestones, such as the selection of a buyer or the completion of regulatory approvals.

- **Addressing Concerns:** Employees will have questions and concerns about how the exit will impact their roles, job security, and benefits. Leadership should be prepared to address these concerns openly and provide as much clarity as possible.

- **Maintaining Focus on Performance:** While the exit process is underway, it's important to keep the company focused on performance. Leaders should remind employees of the company's strategic goals and ensure that day-to-day operations continue smoothly.

2. Retaining Key Talent During the Transition

One of the biggest risks during an exit is the potential loss of key talent. Management and employees may feel uncertain about their future with the company, leading to higher turnover. Retaining key talent during the transition is essential for ensuring operational stability and maintaining the company's value.

Strategies for retaining talent during an exit include:

- **Retention Bonuses:** Offering retention bonuses to key employees can provide an incentive for them to stay through the transition. These bonuses are typically paid out after the exit is complete, ensuring that critical talent remains in place during the most important phases of the process.

- **Clear Career Paths:** For companies being sold to a strategic buyer or merging with another entity, it's important to provide employees with clarity about their future career paths. If possible, leadership should communicate how the transition will provide new opportunities for growth and advancement.

- **Engaging Leadership:** The company's leadership team plays a critical role in keeping employees engaged and motivated during the exit process. Leaders should remain visible, approachable, and supportive, ensuring that employees feel valued and confident about the future.

3. Preparing the Leadership Team for Post-Exit

For members of the leadership team, an exit often signals a significant shift in responsibilities or even a change in ownership. It's important to prepare the leadership team for the next phase of attracting buyers who are looking for a business that can continue growing without needing a complete overhaul. Optimizing supply chains, refining production processes, and eliminating inefficiencies are key steps.

- **Implementing Technology for Scalability:** Companies that have invested in scalable technology platforms, such as enterprise resource planning (ERP) systems, customer relationship management (CRM) tools, or automation technologies, are better positioned for growth. These systems allow companies to scale more efficiently and with fewer operational bottlenecks. Buyers will appreciate companies that have infrastructure in place that can support expansion.

- **Talent and Leadership Strength:** A company's leadership team and workforce are essential to its operational success. Buyers will want to know that the company has a strong management team in place that can continue to run the business effectively post-acquisition. Investing in leadership development, succession planning, and retaining key talent are critical steps in ensuring the company's long-term operational success.

4. Cleaning Up the Balance Sheet

A clean balance sheet, with manageable levels of debt, clear ownership of assets, and minimal liabilities, is highly attractive to potential buyers. Companies preparing for an exit need to ensure that their financial statements are in order and reflect a strong, stable business.

Steps to improve the balance sheet include:

- **Reducing Debt Levels:** High levels of debt can make a company less attractive to buyers, particularly in industries with volatile cash flows. Companies should work to reduce debt levels where possible, either through company's journey, whether that means continuing under new ownership, leading through a merger, or transitioning to a publicly traded entity. Preparing the leadership team for the post-exit environment ensures continuity, smooth integration, and ongoing success.

5. Defining Leadership Roles Post-Exit

One of the key challenges during an exit is determining what the leadership team's roles will look like post-transaction. In some cases, the private equity firm may retain members of the existing leadership team to ensure continuity. In other cases, new leadership may be brought in by the acquiring company or through an IPO process. Defining leadership roles early and clearly can help reduce uncertainty.

Considerations for leadership transitions include:

- **Retaining Key Executives:** If retaining the current leadership team is essential to the success of the business post-exit, private equity firms may negotiate long-term employment contracts or offer retention packages to keep executives in place. This is particularly important in cases where the leadership team's expertise is crucial to maintaining customer relationships or driving future growth.

- **Onboarding New Leaders:** If the company will be bringing in new leadership post-exit (such as a new CEO or CFO in an IPO scenario), a thorough onboarding process is critical.

This helps the new leaders understand the company's culture, values, and strategic direction while integrating them smoothly into the team.

- **Succession Planning:** In situations where certain executives may not stay on post-exit, having a strong succession plan in place ensures there is minimal disruption. Identifying internal talent or planning external hires for key positions can prevent leadership gaps during the transition.

6. Preparing for Cultural and Operational Changes

Each type of exit brings cultural and operational changes, and the leadership team must be prepared to navigate them effectively. Whether the company is merging with another organization, going public, or being acquired by a strategic buyer, these transitions often involve new processes, systems, and expectations.

Key areas of preparation include:

- **Adapting to New Ownership Structures:** In a merger or acquisition, the company may need to integrate with a different organizational culture, adopt new operating procedures, or align with the new parent company's strategic goals. Leaders must be prepared to bridge these cultural and operational differences, ensuring that the integration process is as seamless as possible.

- **Navigating the Public Market:** For companies pursuing an IPO, the shift to becoming a publicly traded company brings new responsibilities, including regulatory compliance, shareholder reporting, and greater scrutiny from analysts and investors. Leaders must be prepared to adapt to these new expectations and manage the complexities of operating in the public market.

- **Maintaining Focus on Core Values:** Amidst the changes that come with an exit, it's essential for leadership to maintain focus on the company's core values and mission. This helps keep employees engaged and ensures that the company's identity remains intact, even as it transitions to new ownership.

7. Providing Leadership Training and Support

The transition period during an exit can be challenging for leaders, particularly if they are facing new expectations, increased scrutiny, or the need to integrate with a larger organization. Providing leadership training and support during this time can help executives and managers navigate the complexities of the exit process and emerge stronger on the other side.

Ways to support leadership development during an exit include:

- **Executive Coaching:** Providing executive coaching during the exit process can help leaders refine their skills, manage stress, and develop strategies for leading their teams through change. Coaching can be particularly valuable in helping executives transition to new roles or responsibilities post-exit.

- **Leadership Workshops:** Offering workshops focused on change management, integration strategies, and public market readiness can equip leaders with the tools they need to navigate the exit. These workshops can also foster collaboration and alignment among the leadership team, ensuring that everyone is working toward the same goals.

- **Peer Networks:** Encouraging leaders to connect with peers who have gone through similar exit processes can provide valuable insights and support. Many private equity firms facilitate networking opportunities among their portfolio companies, allowing leaders to share best practices and learn from each other's experiences.

Workshop Activities

Preparing Management and Employees for Transition

Objective: Explore strategies for preparing management and employees for another transition, ensuring they are informed and motivated throughout the process.

Instructions:

- Create a scenario where a company is preparing for a potential exit, and management and employees are uncertain about their roles and the future of the company.

- Develop a communication and engagement plan that addresses:

  » Transparent communication with management and employees about the upcoming transition.

  » Reassuring key personnel and aligning their goals with the company's objectives during the exit process.

  » Providing support for employees during the transition (e.g., training, counseling, career development opportunities).

  » Ensuring management is aligned with the PE firm's goals and is prepared to guide the company through the transition.

- Write up your communication and engagement plan, explaining how it will prepare management and employees for a smooth transition.

Output: A communication and engagement plan that outlines how management and employees will be prepared and supported during the exit process.

Actionable Takeaway: You will learn how to effectively communicate with and support management and employees during an exit, ensuring that key personnel remain engaged and motivated throughout the process.

Conclusion

Preparing for the next exit is one of the most critical phases of private equity ownership, and how well a company manages this transition will have a lasting impact on its future success. Whether the company is preparing for an IPO, a sale, or a merger, positioning the business for a successful exit requires careful planning, strategic focus, and strong leadership. By understanding the exit strategy, strengthening financial and operational performance, and preparing management and employees for the transition, companies can maximize their value and ensure a smooth exit. Most importantly, leadership must remain focused on maintaining the company's culture, values, and long-term vision throughout the process, setting the stage for continued growth and success after the PE firm exits. The next phase of the company's journey offers new opportunities, and with the right preparation, the business can continue to thrive in the post-exit world.

CHAPTER 16

Long-Term Value Creation Beyond The Exit

> **"**
>
> *Sustaining growth beyond the exit means building resilience, fostering adaptability, and continuously creating long-term value.*
>
> **"**

The journey of a company doesn't end with the exit of a private equity (PE) firm; it often marks the beginning of new challenges. Post-exit, sustaining growth requires a strategic mindset, resilience, and adaptability to new market conditions. This can involve transitioning to public ownership after an IPO, integrating into a larger organization post-sale, or operating under new financial management. This chapter explores strategies for maintaining long-term value creation and competitive edge, building resilience, and adapting to new realities. It also includes lessons from companies that have thrived post-transition, offering insights into continuous success in a dynamic landscape.

Sustaining Growth Post-Exit

The exit of a private equity firm marks a pivotal point in a company's lifecycle. After the exit, the company must continue to grow and create value, often without the close oversight and support that the PE firm provided during its ownership period. To sustain growth, companies need to build on the momentum generated during the PE phase while developing their own internal capabilities to drive future expansion.

1. Focusing on Operational Excellence

During the private equity ownership period, many companies undergo significant operational improvements aimed at increasing efficiency, reducing costs, and boosting profitability. Post-exit, it's important for companies to continue this focus on operational excellence.

Key strategies for maintaining operational excellence include:

- **Continuous Improvement:** Even after the exit, companies should continue to adopt a culture of continuous improvement. This means regularly evaluating processes, systems, and workflows to identify areas for optimization. Companies can implement lean methodologies, automation, and process standardization to ensure that they remain agile and efficient.

- **Scaling Operations:** As the company grows post-exit, it's important to ensure that operations can scale in line with increasing demand. This may involve investing in new technologies, expanding production capabilities, or upgrading infrastructure to support larger volumes of business. Ensuring that operations can scale smoothly is essential to sustaining long-term growth.

- **Talent Development:** Post-exit, the company must continue to invest in its workforce to drive operational success. This involves developing leadership talent, training employees on new technologies or processes, and ensuring that the company has the skills and expertise needed to meet future challenges.

2. Expanding Product Lines and Services

Post-exit, companies often need to explore new avenues for growth. Expanding product lines and services can help companies tap into new revenue streams, increase customer loyalty, and capture additional market share.

Steps to expand product lines and services include:

- **Customer-Centric Innovation:** Companies should continue to innovate by focusing on the needs and preferences of their customers. This involves gathering feedback, conducting market research, and identifying gaps in the market that the company can fill with new products or services. Innovation should be driven by a deep understanding of the customer base and a commitment to delivering value.

- **Cross-Selling and Upselling Opportunities:** Post-exit, companies can focus on expanding their product or service offerings to existing customers. This can include cross-selling complementary products or upselling premium services that enhance the customer experience. By deepening relationships with current customers, companies can generate additional revenue and strengthen customer loyalty.

- **Entering New Markets:** Geographic expansion or entering new market segments is another way to drive growth post-exit. This may involve expanding into international markets, targeting new industries, or reaching out to different demographic groups. However, companies must carefully evaluate market entry strategies to ensure they have the resources and capabilities to succeed in new markets.

3. Strengthening Financial Discipline

Post-exit, companies must maintain strong financial discipline to ensure continued profitability and long-term sustainability. Without the oversight of a private equity firm, which often brings a highly structured financial focus, companies must take responsibility for their own financial management.

Key financial strategies include:

- **Cash Flow Management:** Cash flow is critical for funding growth initiatives, investing in innovation, and managing day-to-day operations. Companies should focus on optimizing working capital, reducing unnecessary expenses, and ensuring that they have enough liquidity to support future investments.

- **Prudent Capital Allocation:** Companies must be strategic about how they allocate capital post-exit. This involves carefully evaluating potential investments, whether in R&D, marketing, or acquisitions, and ensuring that every dollar spent contributes to long-term value creation. Maintaining a disciplined approach to capital allocation helps prevent wasteful spending and ensures that resources are used to drive sustainable growth.

- **Cost Control and Margin Management:** To sustain profitability, companies must continue to control costs and manage margins. This means identifying areas where costs can be reduced without sacrificing quality and ensuring that the company maintains healthy margins as it grows.

Building Resilience and Adaptability for Future Success

In a rapidly changing world, companies must be resilient and adaptable to thrive over the long term. This is especially true post-exit, as the company may face new market dynamics, competitive pressures, or economic challenges. Building resilience involves not only preparing for potential disruptions but also fostering a culture that embraces change and innovation.

1. Developing a Strong Leadership Team

A strong leadership team is essential for guiding the company through future challenges and opportunities. Post-exit, the company must ensure that its leadership team is equipped to navigate uncertainty, make strategic decisions, and inspire employees to perform at their best.

Strategies for building resilient leadership include:

- **Succession Planning:** Succession planning ensures that the company has a pipeline of future leaders who can step into key roles as needed. By identifying high-potential employees and providing them with leadership development opportunities, the company can build a deep bench of talent that is ready to take on new challenges.

- **Leadership Agility:** In a fast-paced business environment, leaders must be agile and able to pivot quickly in response to changing circumstances. Providing leadership training focused on decision-making, problem-solving, and adaptability can help leaders navigate uncertainty and drive the company forward in any situation.

- **Empowering Decision-Making:** Empowering leaders at all levels of the organization to make decisions and take ownership of their responsibilities fosters a culture of accountability and resilience. When leaders are empowered, they can respond more effectively to challenges and take proactive steps to ensure the company's success.

2. Fostering a Culture of Innovation

Innovation is key to long-term value creation, and companies must foster a culture that encourages creativity, experimentation, and risk-taking. Post-exit, companies should continue to invest in innovation to stay ahead of competitors and adapt to changing market conditions.

Ways to foster a culture of innovation include:

- **Encouraging Experimentation:** Companies should create an environment where employees feel comfortable experimenting with new ideas and solutions. This involves providing the resources and support needed to test new products, services, or processes, as well as rewarding innovative thinking.

- **Collaborating Across Functions:** Cross-functional collaboration can spark new ideas and drive innovation.

By encouraging teams from different departments—such as R&D, marketing, and operations—to work together, companies can generate fresh perspectives and develop more innovative solutions.

- **Investing in Technology:** Technology is a key enabler of innovation, and companies should continue to invest in the latest tools and platforms to drive efficiency, enhance customer experiences, and enable new business models. Staying at the forefront of technological advancements helps companies remain competitive and resilient in a rapidly changing landscape.

3. Building Operational Flexibility

Operational flexibility is critical to building resilience. Companies that can adapt their operations to meet changing demand, market conditions, or customer needs are better positioned to thrive in both good times and bad.

Strategies for building operational flexibility include:

- **Diversifying the Supply Chain:** A diversified supply chain helps reduce the risk of disruptions caused by natural disasters, geopolitical events, or supplier failures. Companies should work to build a network of suppliers in different regions, ensuring that they have backup options if their primary suppliers are unable to deliver.

- **Flexible Workforce Models:** Companies that adopt flexible workforce models—such as using a mix of full-time employees, contractors, and gig workers—can adapt more easily to fluctuations in demand. This approach allows companies to scale up or down based on market conditions, ensuring that they can respond quickly to new opportunities or challenges.

- **Agile Manufacturing and Operations:** Agile manufacturing and operations allow companies to pivot quickly when demand shifts or new opportunities arise. This may involve implementing just-in-time inventory systems, automating production processes, or using data analytics to optimize decision-making.

Lessons from Companies that Thrived After Multiple Transitions

Many companies have not only survived but thrived after going through multiple ownership transitions, whether through private equity sales, mergers, or IPOs. By studying these companies, we can gain valuable insights into the strategies that drive long-term success, even in the face of significant change.

1. Embracing Change as a Constant

Companies that thrive after multiple transitions understand that change is a constant in today's business environment. Rather than resisting change, these companies embrace it as an opportunity for growth, innovation, and reinvention.

Example: A leading consumer goods company, after undergoing several ownership transitions, embraced change by continually reinventing its product lines to meet evolving customer preferences. Each ownership change brought new leadership and strategic direction, but the company remained flexible and adaptive, resulting in sustained growth and a strong market presence.

2. Maintaining a Strong Company Culture

Companies that thrive after multiple transitions prioritize maintaining a strong and consistent company culture, even as ownership changes. A strong culture helps retain talent, foster innovation, and ensure operational continuity, regardless of who owns the company.

Example: A software company that experienced several buyouts and an eventual IPO maintained its core values of collaboration, customer focus, and innovation throughout each transition. By staying true to its culture, the company was able to retain key talent, continue delivering exceptional products, and grow its customer base, even as it navigated ownership changes.

3. Investing in Long-Term Growth, Not Just Short-Term Gains

Successful companies focus on long-term value creation, even when faced with short-term pressures from new owners or public markets. They prioritize investments in innovation, talent, and operational improvements that drive sustainable growth over time.

Example: A healthcare company that went through multiple private equity buyouts and eventually went public maintained a focus on long-term investments in R&D and technology. Despite the short-term pressures from PE owners and the demands of public investors, the company's commitment to innovation positioned it as a market leader and enabled sustained growth post-IPO.

4. Leveraging Each Transition as a Learning Opportunity

Companies that have thrived through multiple transitions view each ownership change as an opportunity to learn, evolve, and improve. By analyzing what worked and what didn't during previous transitions, these companies continually refine their strategies and become more resilient.

Example: A manufacturing company that experienced several mergers and buyouts used each transition as an opportunity to strengthen its operations and supply chain. By learning from past integration challenges, the company developed best practices for streamlining operations, reducing costs, and maintaining quality, ultimately becoming a leader in its industry.

Workshop Activities

Financial Management for Long-Term Growth

Objective: Develop strategies for managing the company's finances post-exit to support sustainable growth and long-term profitability.

Instructions:

- Develop a fictional company's financial reports, highlighting areas that need improvement (e.g., high debt levels, cash flow challenges, or low profitability).

- Each group is tasked with developing a financial

management strategy that includes:

- » Reducing debt and improving cash flow to strengthen the company's financial position.

- » Allocating capital to high-impact growth initiatives, such as R&D, market expansion, or technology investments.

- » Implementing cost-saving measures to improve profitability without sacrificing quality or innovation.

- » Monitoring key financial metrics to ensure the company remains on track for long-term success.

- Build financial management strategies, detail how these strategies will support the company's long-term growth and profitability.

Output: A financial management strategy that outlines key actions to improve the company's financial health and support sustainable growth.

Actionable Takeaway: You will learn how to manage a company's finances post-exit to ensure long-term growth, profitability, and financial stability.

Conclusion

Long-term value creation goes beyond the exit of a private equity firm. It requires a focus on sustaining growth, building resilience, and adapting to future challenges. Companies that thrive after an exit are those that continue to invest in operational excellence, innovation, and leadership development, while maintaining a flexible, adaptive approach to change.

By studying the lessons of companies that have successfully navigated multiple transitions, we can see that resilience, adaptability, and a commitment to long-term growth are the keys to enduring success. Whether through continuous operational improvements, embracing innovation, or fostering a strong culture, companies can continue to create value and thrive long after their private equity owners have moved on.

CHAPTER 17

Personal Career Growth Post-Acquisition

> *Your private equity experience is the key to unlocking new career opportunities—seize it, grow with it, and make your next move count.*

For employees, particularly executives and key managers, the acquisition by a private equity (PE) firm marks a pivotal career moment. The intense focus on operational improvements, financial performance, and growth under PE ownership can spur professional development and offer invaluable experience. However, the opportunities for career advancement don't end with the PE firm's exit or the company's sale. This chapter discusses how individuals can leverage their experiences post-acquisition to advance their careers, identify new opportunities within and outside the company, and build a strong personal network in the PE world, capitalizing on the unique advantages this period offers.

Leveraging the PE Experience for Career Advancement

Private equity ownership places a premium on performance, operational efficiency, and results-driven leadership. For those who navigate a company through a PE acquisition, these skills become valuable assets in their personal career growth. The fast-paced environment of a PE-owned company provides a unique opportunity to gain experience in areas such as strategic planning, financial analysis, operational improvements, and leadership under pressure.

1. Gaining Operational and Strategic Expertise

Private equity firms are known for their hands-on approach to improving portfolio companies, particularly when it comes to driving operational excellence and implementing strategic initiatives. Executives and managers who have been part of this process gain valuable expertise that can be leveraged in future roles.

Key areas of expertise gained through the PE experience include:

- **Operational Efficiency:** PE-backed companies are often pushed to streamline processes, reduce costs, and improve productivity. Executives who have overseen these efforts develop strong operational management skills, including process optimization, cost control, and the ability to implement lean methodologies.

- **Financial Acumen:** PE firms focus heavily on financial

metrics such as EBITDA, cash flow, and return on investment (ROI). Individuals who have worked in a PE-backed company become proficient in financial analysis, budgeting, and performance tracking, making them attractive candidates for future leadership roles.

- **Strategic Planning:** Under PE ownership, companies are expected to scale quickly and achieve aggressive growth targets. Executives involved in strategic planning gain experience in market analysis, competitive positioning, product development, and M&A activity, all of which are valuable for career advancement.

2. Demonstrating Leadership in High-Pressure Environments

One of the hallmarks of private equity ownership is the pressure to deliver results within a relatively short time frame. Leaders in PE-backed companies must navigate the challenges of scaling the business, meeting financial targets, and managing operational changes—all under the watchful eye of the private equity firm.

Leadership qualities developed in a PE-backed environment include:

- **Decision-Making Under Pressure:** The ability to make sound, data-driven decisions in a high-pressure environment is a critical skill that executives can leverage in future leadership roles. The experience of managing uncertainty and making tough calls during the transition period under PE ownership is highly valued by other organizations.

- **Change Management:** PE firms often drive significant operational changes, including restructuring, new processes, and shifts in strategic focus. Leaders who have successfully managed these transitions gain expertise in change management, employee engagement, and communication, all of which are essential skills for career growth.

- **Accountability and Performance:** In a PE-owned company, there is a strong emphasis on accountability and meeting performance metrics. Executives who have thrived in this environment demonstrate a results-oriented approach and the ability to drive teams toward achieving key objectives.

3. Building a Track Record of Value Creation

Private equity firms invest in companies with the goal of increasing value, and executives who play a key role in driving this value creation can point to tangible results as they pursue new career opportunities. Whether it's improving financial performance, expanding market share, or leading successful product launches, having a track record of value creation is a powerful asset for career advancement.

Leveraging a track record of value creation:

- **Quantifiable Achievements:** Executives should highlight quantifiable achievements from their time at the PE-backed company, such as revenue growth, cost savings, operational improvements, or successful M&A deals. These metrics provide concrete evidence of leadership effectiveness and impact.

- **Communicating Impact:** When seeking new opportunities, it's important to articulate the role played in the company's success during PE ownership. Whether in interviews or on a resume, executives should emphasize how their contributions led to improved performance, enhanced profitability, or strategic growth.

Opportunities Within and

Beyond the Company

The post-acquisition environment offers numerous opportunities for personal career growth, both within the company and beyond. As the company transitions to new ownership, executives and managers can explore different paths for advancing their careers, depending on their goals and interests.

1. Internal Career Opportunities

For individuals who want to continue their career with the company post-acquisition, there may be new roles, responsibilities, or growth opportunities. Whether the company has been sold to a strategic buyer, merged with another organization, or gone public, the transition can open up new leadership positions and pathways for advancement.

Internal career opportunities include:

- **Leadership Roles in the New Organization:** In cases where the company has been acquired by a larger organization, executives and managers may have the opportunity to take on leadership roles within the broader corporate structure. This could include overseeing multiple divisions, expanding into new markets, or managing cross-functional teams.

- **New Responsibilities Post-IPO:** For companies that go public through an IPO, executives often take on new responsibilities related to regulatory compliance, investor relations, and public market strategy. Leaders with experience in financial reporting, governance, and communication can advance their careers in these areas.

- **Driving Post-Acquisition Integration:** For executives who thrive on operational challenges, the post-acquisition period often involves integrating the company's systems, processes, and culture with the acquiring organization. Leading this integration effort can be a valuable experience and position individuals for future leadership roles.

2. Opportunities Beyond the Company

For those seeking new opportunities beyond the company, the experience gained during a private equity acquisition can serve as a launching pad for new career paths. Many executives leverage their PE experience to pursue roles in other PE-backed companies, corporate leadership, or entrepreneurial ventures.

Opportunities beyond the company include:

- **Moving to Another PE-Backed Company:** Executives who have successfully navigated a private equity acquisition are highly sought after by other PE firms. They bring a deep understanding of the PE model, including the focus on operational improvements, financial performance, and growth strategy. Many individuals choose to take on leadership roles in other PE portfolio companies, where they can apply their skills in a new context.

- **C-Suite Roles in Public or Private Companies:** The strategic, financial, and operational experience gained in a PE-backed company makes executives attractive candidates for C-suite roles in both public and private companies. Whether pursuing a CEO, COO, or CFO role, individuals can leverage their leadership track record to secure top positions in other organizations.

- **Entrepreneurial Ventures:** Some executives choose to use their PE experience as a springboard for entrepreneurship. The skills developed in managing growth, optimizing operations, and driving financial performance are invaluable for launching and scaling a new business. Additionally, connections made in the PE world can provide access to investors, mentors, and advisors for those looking to start their own company.

3. Serving as a Board Member or Advisor

For executives looking to broaden their impact beyond a single organization, serving as a board member or advisor can be an excellent way to leverage their experience in private equity and corporate leadership. Many PE firms and corporate boards seek individuals with deep operational, financial, and strategic expertise to provide guidance and oversight.

Opportunities in board and advisory roles include:

- **Joining Corporate Boards:** Many executives who have successfully led PE-backed companies are invited to join the boards of other companies. Board roles allow individuals to provide strategic oversight, mentor senior leaders, and help guide the company's long-term vision.

- **Advising PE Firms and Portfolio Companies:** PE firms often seek out experienced executives to serve as advisors to their portfolio companies. These advisory roles involve providing guidance on operational improvements, growth strategies, and financial performance. Advisors may also assist with due diligence on potential investments or provide mentorship to management teams.

- **Consulting Opportunities:** For those looking to share their expertise without committing to full-time roles, consulting offers a flexible way to contribute to multiple organizations. Executives can work as independent consultants, offering their insights and experience to help companies navigate transitions, improve performance, or execute growth strategies.

Building a Personal Network in the PE World

One of the most valuable assets that individuals can cultivate during and after a private equity acquisition is a strong professional network. The private equity world is highly interconnected, and building relationships with PE professionals, other portfolio company executives, and industry experts can open doors to new opportunities, partnerships, and career advancement.

1. Networking with PE Professionals

Private equity firms are constantly looking for experienced executives to lead their portfolio companies, advise on investment opportunities, or assist with operational improvements. Developing relationships with PE professionals—such as managing directors, partners, and operating partners—can provide access to new career opportunities within the PE ecosystem.

Strategies for networking with PE professionals:

- **Stay Connected with the PE Firm:** Even after an exit, maintaining relationships with the private equity firm that acquired your company can be valuable. Many PE firms have multiple portfolio companies, and executives who have successfully led one company through a PE acquisition are often considered for leadership roles at other portfolio companies.

- **Attend PE Industry Conferences and Events:** Private equity conferences, summits, and networking events provide opportunities to meet PE professionals, share insights, and build relationships. These events can also be a platform for executives to showcase their expertise and position themselves for future opportunities.

- **Leverage PE Relationships for Mentorship:** PE professionals often have extensive experience in corporate leadership, finance, and strategy. Building mentor relationships with individuals in the PE world can provide guidance, feedback, and support as you navigate your own career growth.

2. Building Relationships with Other Portfolio Company Executives

In addition to networking with private equity professionals, it's important to build relationships with other executives who have led or are currently leading PE-backed companies. These individuals have a shared understanding of the unique challenges and opportunities that come with private equity ownership and can provide valuable insights and connections.

Ways to build relationships with other portfolio company executives:

- **Participate in Portfolio Company Events:** Many PE firms host events, such as CEO summits, roundtable discussions, or portfolio company conferences, where executives can meet and collaborate with their peers. These events provide an opportunity to share best practices, discuss common challenges, and build a supportive network.

- **Join Industry Associations or Networks:** Industry associations, peer groups, and executive networks are excellent ways to connect with other leaders in your field. Joining these organizations allows you to expand your network, stay updated on industry trends, and gain exposure to new career opportunities.

- **Collaborate on Cross-Portfolio Initiatives:** Some private equity firms encourage collaboration across their portfolio companies, whether through shared services, joint ventures, or operational best practices. Engaging in these initiatives allows executives to build relationships with their peers while contributing to the success of other portfolio companies.

3. Leveraging Social Media and Online Platforms

In today's digital age, building a personal brand and expanding your network through online platforms is more important than ever. Social media, particularly LinkedIn, offers executives a powerful tool for connecting with other professionals, sharing insights, and building visibility in the private equity space.

Strategies for building an online network:

- **Optimize Your LinkedIn Profile:** Your LinkedIn profile should clearly communicate your expertise, accomplishments, and career goals. Highlight your experience in leading PE-backed companies, your track record of value creation, and your leadership skills. An optimized profile makes it easier for PE firms and recruiters to find you and consider you for future roles.

- **Engage with Thought Leadership:** Posting articles, sharing industry insights, and engaging in discussions on LinkedIn or other professional platforms can help you establish yourself as a thought leader in your field. Contributing to conversations around private equity, corporate leadership, or industry-specific topics helps build your credibility and expands your network.

- **Join Online Groups and Communities:** LinkedIn and other platforms host numerous groups and communities focused on private equity, leadership, and industry-specific discussions. Joining these groups allows you to connect with like-minded professionals, stay informed on the latest trends, and build relationships with key players in the PE world.

Workshop Activities

Creating a Personal Brand

Objective: Learn how to create a strong personal brand that reflects participants' skills, experiences, and value in the job market, particularly in the context of working in a PE-backed company.

Instructions:

- Develop your personal brand statement showing how you have successfully leveraged your private equity experience to advance your career.

- Task yourself with:

  » Defining your unique value proposition based on the skills, achievements, and experiences gained in a post-acquisition environment.

  » Crafting your personal brand statement that clearly communicates your expertise and how you can add value to potential employers or clients.

  » Update your LinkedIn profiles or personal websites to reflect your personal brand, showcasing their accomplishments and thought leadership.

- Show your personal brand statements to a few friends to get feedvback.

Output: A personal brand statement and updated LinkedIn profile that highlights participants' unique skills and value in the job market, particularly in the private equity or post-acquisition space.

Actionable Takeaway: You will learn how to create and refine a personal brand that clearly communicates your value, positioning yourself as an attractive candidate for new opportunities in the job market.

Conclusion

The experience gained during a private equity acquisition is an invaluable asset for personal career growth. Whether leveraging operational expertise, demonstrating leadership under pressure, or building a track record of value creation, executives and managers who have successfully navigated a PE-owned company are well-positioned for future success. By exploring internal opportunities within the company, seeking new roles in the broader private equity ecosystem, or transitioning to advisory and board positions, individuals can capitalize on the skills and insights gained during the acquisition. Additionally, building a strong personal network within the PE world—both with PE professionals and other portfolio company executives—can open doors to new opportunities and ensure continued career growth. Ultimately, private equity offers a unique environment for professional development, and those who embrace the challenges and opportunities presented by a PE acquisition can advance their careers in meaningful and rewarding ways.

BUILDING A FUTURE OF SUCCESS AFTER PRIVATE EQUITY

Congratulations! If you've made it this far, you are well-equipped with the knowledge, tools, and insights to thrive in the fast-paced, ever-evolving world of private equity. Whether you're a leader, a key employee, or part of the workforce navigating a PE acquisition, you've been through a unique and transformative experience—one that can position you and your company for long-term success.

The journey we've explored throughout this book—understanding private equity, managing transitions, scaling for growth, and preparing for the exit—culminates in one central truth: private equity is a catalyst for change. It challenges companies to think bigger, move faster, and operate smarter. But the power of private equity goes beyond financial performance. It's about building stronger, more resilient companies, and creating environments where innovation, growth, and success thrive.

Now that you've gained a deeper understanding of the private equity process, it's time to apply what you've learned to continuously improve your company, uplift your co-workers, and prepare for a future full of opportunities.

Embrace Change and Focus on Continuous Improvement

Change is inevitable in the private equity world, but instead of fearing it, learn to embrace it. Companies that thrive post-acquisition are those that welcome change and use it as a driver for continuous improvement. No matter where your company stands, there's always room to innovate, optimize, and grow.

Here's how you can embrace continuous improvement:

- **Foster a Growth Mindset:** Encourage your team to view challenges as opportunities for growth. Cultivate a mindset that sees obstacles as stepping stones to greater success. When you and your team approach each day with the belief that there's always something to learn or improve, you unlock a culture of innovation and progress.

- **Adopt Best Practices:** You've learned about operational efficiency, strategic planning, and financial discipline. Now it's time to implement these best practices across your organization. Whether you're streamlining processes, managing cash flow, or finding new ways to create value for customers, aim to make incremental improvements that build toward long-term success.

- **Invest in Your People:** Your employees are your greatest asset. Continuously invest in their development, whether through training programs, leadership opportunities, or mentorship. A motivated, skilled workforce will drive the company's future growth and ensure it can adapt to whatever lies ahead.

Motivate and Empower Your Team

As you've seen, navigating private equity isn't just about the bottom line—it's about people. Your company's success depends on a team that is motivated, engaged, and empowered to contribute their best. As a leader, colleague, or contributor, you have the power to inspire others to rise to new heights and achieve great things together.

Inspire your co-workers by:

- **Setting Clear Goals and Communicating Vision:** People perform best when they understand the company's direction and their role in achieving it. Set ambitious, yet attainable goals, and ensure that everyone knows how their contributions make an impact. A shared vision unites your team and gives them a sense of purpose.

- **Celebrating Wins—Big and Small:** Recognize the efforts of your team, whether it's hitting a key milestone, completing a major project, or simply showing dedication in their daily work. Celebrating both the big successes and the small, incremental wins keeps morale high and motivates your team to keep pushing forward.

- **Encouraging Collaboration and Innovation:** Break down silos and encourage open communication and collaboration across departments. Teams that work together creatively to solve problems and share knowledge are more likely to generate innovative solutions that move the company ahead.

Lead with Optimism

and Resilience

One of the most valuable lessons from the private equity experience is the importance of resilience. Market conditions, industry dynamics, and economic shifts may create uncertainties, but with the right mindset, your company can weather any storm. Optimism, paired with strategic resilience, will guide you through challenges and help you see opportunities in even the toughest situations.

To lead with optimism and resilience:

- **Stay Adaptable:** The ability to pivot, rethink strategies, and embrace new opportunities is essential in today's dynamic business world. Be open to evolving circumstances, whether it's adapting to new market trends, shifting customer demands, or operational challenges. Flexibility is the key to thriving in times of change.

- **Keep a Long-Term Vision:** While private equity may have focused on short-term results, don't lose sight of the long-term goals of your company. Continue investing in innovation, technology, and talent to ensure your business remains competitive and resilient in the years ahead. A strong vision will serve as your north star as you guide your company through future transitions.

- **Cultivate Optimism:** A positive attitude is contagious. When you approach challenges with optimism, it encourages your team to stay motivated and committed, even when the road gets tough. Optimism breeds confidence, and confidence fuels action.

Final Words of Encouragement

The private equity process is demanding, but it's also a powerful opportunity for transformation. Your company has undergone changes, but it has also grown stronger, more efficient, and more agile. As you move forward, take pride in the journey you and your team have been on. You've acquired new skills, developed resilience, and proven that your company can rise to the occasion.

Remember, the future belongs to those who are willing to embrace it with open minds and full hearts. Whether your company is growing, merging, or facing new challenges, you have the tools and the mindset to lead it toward continued success.

Now, go out and build a future that you and your team can be proud of. Continue to innovate, inspire, and create lasting value—not only for your company but for the people who work beside you. This is just the beginning of an exciting new chapter, and you have the power to shape it.

Stay optimistic, stay resilient, and never stop moving forward. The best is yet to come!

APPENDIX: FURTHER READING BY CHAPTER TOPICS

Chapter 1: What is Private Equity?

- *Private Equity: History, Governance, and Operations* – **Harry Cendrowski** (2012)
- *The Masters of Private Equity and Venture Capital* – **Robert Finkel** (2009)
- *King of Capital* – **David Carey** (2010)

Chapter 2: The Buyout Process Unveiled

- *Investment Banks, Hedge Funds, and Private Equity* – **David Stowell** (2012)
- *Barbarians at the Gate* – **Bryan Burrough** (1990)
- *Private Equity Operational Due Diligence* – **Jason Scharfman** (2018)

Chapter 3: Why Companies Are Acquired by PE

- *The Private Equity Playbook* – **Adam Coffey** (2019)
- *Corporate Restructuring: Lessons from Experience* – **Stuart Slatter** (2006)
- *Good to Great* – **Jim Collins** (2001)

Chapter 4: The First 100 Days Post-Acquisition

- *The First 90 Days* – **Michael D. Watkins** (2013)
- *Extreme Ownership* – **Jocko Willink** (2015)
- *The Hard Thing About Hard Things* – **Ben Horowitz** (2014)

Chapter 5: Navigating Cultural Shifts

- *The Culture Code* – **Daniel Coyle** (2018)
- *Switch: How to Change Things When Change Is Hard* – **Chip Heath & Dan Heath** (2010)
- *Drive: The Surprising Truth About What Motivates Us* – **Daniel H. Pink** (2009)

Chapter 6: Re-Defining Roles and Responsibilities

- *Radical Candor* – **Kim Scott** (2017)
- *Leaders Eat Last* – **Simon Sinek** (2014)
- *Dare to Lead* – **Brené Brown** (2018)

Chapter 7: Performance Metrics and Accountability

- *Measure What Matters* – **John Doerr** (2018)
- *The Balanced Scorecard* – **Robert S. Kaplan** (1996)
- *What the CEO Wants You to Know* – **Ram Charan** (2001)

Chapter 8: Operational Improvements and Cost Efficiency

- *The Lean Startup* – **Eric Ries** (2011)
- *The Goal: A Process of Ongoing Improvement* – **Eliyahu M. Goldratt** (1984)
- *Lean Thinking* – **James P. Womack** (1996)

Chapter 9: Talent Management and Retention Strategies

- *The Five Dysfunctions of a Team* – **Patrick Lencioni** (2002)
- *Work Rules!* – **Laszlo Bock** (2015)

- *First, Break All the Rules* – **Marcus Buckingham** (1999)

Chapter 10: Strategies for Scaling the Business

- *Scaling Up* – **Verne Harnish** (2014)
- *Blitzscaling* – **Reid Hoffman** (2018)
- *HBR Guide to Growing Your Business* – **Harvard Business Review** (2018)

Chapter 11: Leveraging the PE Network

- *Networking Like a Pro* – **Ivan R. Misner** (2017)
- *Give and Take* – **Adam Grant** (2013)
- *Private Equity Operational Improvement* – **Johan Ericsson** (2012)

Chapter 12: Innovating Under New Ownership

- *The Innovator's Dilemma* – **Clayton M. Christensen** (1997)
- *Blue Ocean Strategy* – **W. Chan Kim & Renée Mauborgne** (2005)
- *Creative Confidence* – **Tom Kelley & David Kelley** (2013)

Chapter 13: Dealing with Difficult People

- *Crucial Conversations* – **Kerry Patterson** (2012)
- *The No Asshole Rule* – **Robert I. Sutton** (2007)
- *Difficult Conversations* – **Douglas Stone** (2010)

Chapter 14: Helping People Make Decisions

- *Decisive: How to Make Better Choices* – **Chip Heath & Dan Heath** (2013)

- *Thinking, Fast and Slow* – **Daniel Kahneman** (2011)
- *Nudge: Improving Decisions About Health, Wealth, and Happiness* – **Richard H. Thaler** (2008)

Chapter 15: Preparing for the Next Exit

- *Built to Sell* – **John Warrillow** (2010)
- *The Art of Selling Your Business* – **John Warrillow** (2021)
- *Harvesting Intangible Assets* – **Andrew J. Sherman** (2011)

Chapter 16: Long-Term Value Creation Beyond the Exit

- *Great by Choice* – **Jim Collins** (2011)
- *The Outsiders* – **William N. Thorndike** (2012)
- *Good Profit* – **Charles G. Koch** (2015)

Chapter 17: Personal Career Growth Post-Acquisition

- *So Good They Can't Ignore You* – **Cal Newport** (2012)
- *Grit: The Power of Passion and Perseverance* – **Angela Duckworth** (2016)
- *Pivot: The Only Move That Matters Is Your Next One* – **Jenny Blake** (2016)

Bonus: Books to Elevate Your Dinner Party Conversations

- *"Capitalism and Freedom"* - **Milton Friedman**, 1962
- *"Free to Choose: A Personal Statement"* - **Milton Friedman and Rose Friedman**, 1980
- *"The Tyranny of the Status Quo"* - **Milton Friedman and Rose Friedman**, 1984

- *"Price Theory"* - **Milton Friedman** (Year of publication varies by edition)

- *"Money Mischief: Episodes in Monetary History"* - **Milton Friedman**, 1992

- *"Why Government is the Problem"* - **Milton Friedman**, 1993

Thank you for reading, and here's to your ongoing success!

About The Author

Mort Greenberg brings over 25 years of experience as a business leader, working with tech start-ups and major media companies. Rising from an Account Executive to the President of a division with 800+ employees generating $220 million in annual revenue, Mort has supported revenue efforts for various companies as they navigated the need for growth, mergers, acquisitions, and IPOs. He was instrumental in shaping the digital advertising landscape during the early days of the Internet at Excite.com and Ask Jeeves. He has also held leadership roles at IAC / InterActive-Corp, NBC Universal, Nokia, and iHeartMedia. Along the way, he launched two companies of his own, FitAd and MindFlight, and learned that start-ups are not always successful. Since 2016, he has been helping turn around distressed media properties into profitable companies for a global private equity firm. The #1 lesson he has learned in all his years is that by improving people's revenue mindset, business problems are healed, and teams are motivated through innovation that new revenue affords.